Labor Agreement Negotiations
7ᵗʰ Edition

Edwin C. Leonard, Jr.
Professor of Business Administration
School of Business and Management Sciences
Indiana University Purdue University Fort Wayne (IPFW)

Claire McCarty Kilian
Assistant Professor of Business Administration
College of Business & Economics
University of Wisconsin – River Falls

Raymond L. Hilgert
Professor Emeritus of Management and Industrial Relations
John M. Olin School of Business
Washington University – St. Louis, MO

THOMSON
CUSTOM PUBLISHING

Editor: Greg Albert
Publishing Services Supervisor: Christina Smith
Manufacturing Supervisor: Becky Schwartz
Graphic Designer: Krista Pierson
Rights and Permissions Specialist: Kalina Ingham Hintz
Project Coordinator: Brian Schaefer
Marketing Manager: Sara L. Hinckley

Printed in the United States of America

Thomson Custom Publishing
5191 Natorp Blvd.
Mason, Ohio 45040
USA

For information about our products, contact us:
1-800-355-9983
http://www.thomsoncustom.com

International Headquarters
Thomson Learning
International Division
290 Harbor Drive, 2nd Floor
Stamford, CT 06902-7477
USA

UK/Europe/Middle East/South Africa
Thomson Learning
Berkshire House
168-173 High Holborn
London WCIV 7AA

Asia
Thomson Learning
60 Albert Street, #15-01
Albert Complex
Singapore 189969

Canada
Nelson Thomson Learning
1120 Birchmount Road
Toronto, Ontario MIK 5G4
Canada
United Kingdom

Visit us at www.thomsoncustom.com and learn more about this book and other titles published by Thomson Learning Custom Publishing

0-759-31314-8

The Adaptable Courseware Program consists of products and additions to existing Custom Publishing products that are produced from camera-ready copy. Peer review, class testing, and accuracy are primarily the responsibility of the author(s).

PREFACE

Labor Agreement Negotiations provides a convenient but challenging set of materials for students to use in a realistic simulation of union-management negotiations. As an experiential approach, it is most appropriate for survey or advanced courses in human resource management, collective bargaining and labor relations, labor economics, or labor law, either at the undergraduate or graduate level. It also could be used in courses on conflict resolution, and it is suitable for conferences or seminars designed to develop negotiating skills of practitioners in the field, such as supervisors, managers, human resource professionals, and union leaders.

Labor Agreement Negotiations is based on materials that were collected and developed from an actual union-management negotiation. The names of the company, union, and all individuals are disguised. Data and issues have been added and updated from previous versions in order to make the simulation experience relevant to today's environment. Students who participate in this simulated negotiation will find it to be a stimulating and rewarding learning experience.

An Instructor's Manual (IM) is available to assist the instructor in planning and supervising the simulation. The IM contains the authors' comments and suggested approaches, including optional variations for conducting the simulation. The manual also includes:

- ✓ A number of useful forms to help participants prepare for and conduct their negotiations.
- ✓ A computer application program that instructors may provide to negotiating teams if they choose.
- ✓ An electronic copy of the current contract.
- ✓ Several evaluation forms useful for discussion and grading purposes.
- ✓ Pre-negotiation exercises.
- ✓ Sample exam questions.
- ✓ A list of video and reading resources.

The instructor may adapt any or all of these materials according to his or her specific needs and preferences. However, the suggested scheduling formats should be followed as closely as possible, because the sequencing outlined here is pedagogically effective.

This edition could not have been written and published without the generous, expert assistance of many people. We have benefited from the contributions of those who made previous versions of the simulation an effective learning tool. We are grateful to the many people who contributed to this seventh edition. Our sincere appreciation goes to Jan Tiefel of JKL Publishers for her support and encouragement. Jayla Heller of IPFW poured hours into correcting and processing the final draft. Many students, faculty, and staff members have been involved in helping us to update the simulation and enhance the Instructor's Manual for this edition. We would specifically like to thank Janet Papiernik, IPFW, for her assistance with the financial reports; Valerie Richardson, IPFW, for her ability to find demographic data; and Charles Yoos, Fort Lewis College, for his suggestions. We'd also like to acknowledge the thorough, constructive reviews that we've received from other faculty that suggested areas for improvement and additional emphasis. Together with past contributors, they have helped us to create an exciting, flexible and relevant simulation.

The 7th edition of Labor Agreement Negotiations is a continuation of previous editions authored by Professor Raymond Hilgert. We have benefited from the conscientious development that was laid down in earlier editions and continued through this edition. Ray, we appreciate your past contributions and dedicate this edition to you.

Spring 2003   Edwin C. Leonard, Jr.   Claire McCarty Kilian

 # ABOUT THE AUTHORS

Dr. Edwin C. Leonard, Jr., is Professor of Business Administration at Indiana University Purdue University Fort Wayne (IPFW). He received his Bachelor's, Master's, and Doctor's degrees from Purdue University. Since joining Indiana University more than 30 years ago, he has held a variety of faculty and administrative positions, including serving as chair of the Management and Marketing Department in the School of Business and Management Sciences. Dr. Leonard has designed and conducted workshops and seminars for thousands of supervisors and managers. Dr. Leonard currently serves as academic advisor and coordinator of Do-it-Best Corp's Retail Management Training Course; this comprehensive program is for management personnel of one of the nation's largest hardware and building materials retailers.

Dr. Leonard's primary research interests are in the areas of human resource management interventions, employee involvement, teaming, organizational climate and leadership, and case development. He has published in a variety of academic and professional journals including *The Journal of Collective Bargaining in the Public Sector*, instructional supplement manuals, and proceedings. He is editor of the *Business Case Journal*. He has authored or co-authored four books dealing with supervisory and human resource issues. Dr. Leonard has held numerous offices in national and regional professional organizations. His professional memberships include the Society for Case Research, the Midwest Society for Human Resources/Industrial Relations, the Organizational Behavior Teaching Society, and the North American Case Research Association.

Dr. Leonard has extensive teaching experience in the Human Resources/Labor Relations area. He served on the Indiana Education Employees Relations Board and has taught Fundamentals of Collective Bargaining for the Indiana University Labor Education and Research Center. Dr. Leonard was the recipient of the National University Continuing Education Association's Service Award for Continuing Education for the Professions, and he received the Award of Teaching Excellence from the Indiana University School of Continuing Studies. Dr. Leonard has received several "best paper" and "distinguished case" awards from various organizations.

Dr. Claire McCarty Kilian is Assistant Professor of Business Administration in the College of Business & Economics at the University of Wisconsin – River Falls. She earned her doctorate in Labor & Human Resources at The Ohio State University and received a B.A. degree in Psychology and Anthropology from the University of Wisconsin – Madison. She has taught graduate and undergraduate courses in management and human resources for over seventeen years at a number of institutions and has published in the *Labor Law Journal, Research in Personnel and Human Resources Management*, several cases in the *Annual Advances in Business*

Cases, and the *T+D Magazine* (formerly *Training & Development*). Her primary research areas are in employee recognition, negotiation/persuasion, team learning, and case development.

Dr. Kilian bridges the gap between management theory and management practice by consulting with organizations providing relevant, practical management information, tools, and techniques. She has developed and facilitated several Supervisory Management Workshops for the University of Wisconsin System. She has also developed the Coach Guide and Workshop for the *Team Learning Lab*, a video-supported (featuring Peter Senge, author of the best-selling book *The Fifth Discipline*) organizational learning program designed as a practice field for teams. Dr. Kilian co-developed and facilitated *Organizational Influence and Work/Life*, part of a Certificate Program for Boston College and the Alliance of Work/Life Professionals (AWLP).

Dr. Kilian's professional memberships include the American Society for Training & Development (a former chapter president), Society for Human Resource Management, Academy of Management, Society for Case Research, and the Organization for the Study of Communication, Language, and Gender. She is experienced in using and developing cases, simulations, and experiential exercises.

Dr. Raymond L. Hilgert is Professor Emeritus of Management and Industrial Relations at the Olin School of Business of Washington University. He graduated from Westminster College, Fulton, Missouri, with a Bachelor of Arts Degree, and received his Master's and Doctor's degrees from Washington University. His business experience includes management positions at Southwestern Bell Telephone Company and a market research position with an advertising company. Dr. Hilgert taught at Washington University for some 40 years, including serving as Assistant Dean and Director of Management Development Programs. He has published over 90 articles and has authored or co-authored six books on human resource management, collective bargaining, industrial relations, and business ethics, three of which are in the sixth, eighth, and tenth editions.

Dr. Hilgert has been a member of the Academy of Management, the Industrial Relations Research Association, the Society for Human Resource Management, the American Compensation Association, and the American Management Association. He has participated in or directed numerous management, supervisory, and business ethics programs and seminars. As an arbitrator certified by the Federal Mediation and Conciliation Service, Dr. Hilgert heard and decided hundreds of union/management grievance-arbitration cases. He holds the Senior Professional in Human Resources (SPHR) accreditation from the Personnel Accreditation Institute. He has received a number of teaching awards from students at Washington University.

TABLE OF CONTENTS

# SIMULATION PURPOSE AND OBJECTIVES

Students who take courses in human resource management, labor relations and collective bargaining seldom have a realistic opportunity to apply their textbook knowledge to actual union-management bargaining situations. However, the simulated conditions provided in *Labor Agreement Negotiations* offer an excellent opportunity to develop understanding and practical skills in the collective bargaining process of contract negotiations.

Based upon actual negotiations between management and union collective bargaining teams, *Labor Agreement Negotiations* can be used within the classroom, workshop, or laboratory setting as a valuable learning technique. Each participant is part of a union or management team and has an important role in developing and carrying out the bargaining strategy of his or her team.

In actual practice, union and management teams usually negotiate labor agreements with a deadline in mind, including the possibility of a work stoppage if they fail to reach a contract settlement. Consequently, both parties usually set bargaining objectives in advance and try to develop a team strategy for obtaining their goals. In this simulation, too, bargaining teams must:

1. Identify issues and objectives most important to the team and assign a priority or value to each.
2. Analyze their team's position and compile supporting data.
3. Anticipate and be ready to respond to issues felt to be most important by the other party..
4. Develop bargaining strategies, including the limits to which the team can accommodate the other party's bargaining positions.
5. Work together as a team in order to present a uniform consensus on issues.

After completing the preliminary steps, the teams meet to negotiate a new contract. This simulation is designed to replicate the types of actual experiences, including anxieties and frustrations that professionals in the field of labor relations encounter. When the simulation is completed, each participant will have first-hand experience of the mechanics and processes of collective bargaining regardless of the outcome. Participants will also develop interpersonal tools and skills that they can transfer to other types of situations involving real-life negotiations and confrontations with individuals and groups.

 # SIMULATION FORMAT

The instructor will determine the format and timetable for the simulation. On the following pages, three models are suggested for conducting the simulation. The first is a format in which negotiations take place over a number of weeks, using several hours for each session. The second is a more concentrated format in which negotiations are held on a continuous basis over two or more days. The third is an example of an accelerated approach – conducting a successful negotiation simulation in fewer than eight hours. The approximate suggested time frames are logical but flexible departure points that can be modified to fit various class situations.

Regardless of the format chosen, at the end of the first meeting, each participant should be assigned to a team,[1] be aware of the purpose and meeting times of future sessions, and understand the general background and guidelines for the collective bargaining simulation. The first session should allow time to review the simulation materials, to respond to student questions, and to make and clarify any modifications that are agreed upon.

It is vital that all participants study the source materials in considerable depth prior to the sessions. Familiarity with the problems and issues to be negotiated is essential if each participant is to be a valuable team member in developing bargaining proposals and positions. For convenience, much of the cost and research data, preliminary discussions, and demographic and personal information appear in the text, tables, and charts. In actual contract negotiations, many months of work go into collecting information and data, identifying issues likely to be negotiated, preparing arguments to counter the opposition, and developing strategies and counterstrategies. Thus it is essential that each team member be well prepared in this preliminary work so as to contribute to the team's effectiveness and efficient performance.

At the first team planning session, each participant should be assigned a specific role. A number of possible roles are listed on page 7. These can be adapted according to the preferences and number of persons available for each team. It is desirable for each team to select a chief negotiator and to assign and clarify the roles and duties of other participants. Team members must then pool their information and opinions and try to reach a consensus as to the positions and strategies that their team will employ. Most of this work should be accomplished during one or more team meetings before the first negotiating session, so that negotiating time can be used to refine rather than to define the team's initial bargaining posture. It is particularly useful for each team to attempt to estimate the actual costs of various wage and benefit proposals that are likely to be forthcoming in negotiations using the data and information provided.

At the first bargaining session, both negotiating teams present their proposals. Then each team separately participates in a strategy meeting (a caucus) to react to and review its counterpart's positions and the possible strengths and weaknesses therein. Each team should try

---

[1] The Instructor's Manual contains suggestions to determine how assignments can be made.

to evaluate and set priorities concerning the opponent's demands and proposals and identify areas of major and minor differences as well as areas of overlap. With this in mind, each team can restudy cost and other estimates and plan strategy for the next bargaining session. This strategy includes arguments, denials, counterproposals, and areas of agreement or compromise.

The simulation is adaptable for a number of bargaining sessions as class time and the instructor's preferences dictate. Whatever the format, some six to twelve hours of bargaining time are desirable to allow for sufficient team strategy and caucus sessions.[2] Further, the teams will be negotiating with a "strike deadline" in mind; that is, if the parties fail to reach an agreement in the allotted time, it is assumed that the union will strike to further its demands. *The strike deadline may be extended only by permission of the instructor upon the mutual request of both teams.* It can be anticipated that, throughout the bargaining sessions, negotiators will extensively employ debating skills and some of the negotiations techniques identified on pages 61- 64. Periodic caucuses of limited duration to react to issues or to consider compromises are desirable for each team.

At the final session, participants and the instructor evaluate the process of negotiations, the problems encountered, the strategies followed, and the contract settlement, if any is reached. The Instructor's Manual contains several individual and group evaluation forms that can be used to aid in the analysis of the simulation process. The post-session will elicit considerable discussion and insights into how and why individual and group personalities influenced the negotiating process and outcomes. It will also stimulate discussion on strategies that lead to success and/or failure, the need to anticipate the strategies of the counterpart negotiating team, and especially ways to negotiate more effectively in future encounters.

---

[2]In this regard, the requirements of Section 8(d) of the National Labor Relations Act, as amended by the Labor Management Relations (Taft-Hartley) Act, should be understood and followed by the negotiating teams. This law requires both an employer and a union in bargaining to meet at reasonable times and confer in good faith with respect to wages, hours, and other terms and conditions of employment or the negotiation of an agreement or any question arising thereunder, and the execution of a written contract incorporating any agreement reached if requested by either party, but such obligation does not compel either party to agree to a proposal or require the making of a concession. For more detailed information visit: http://hcl.chass.ncsu.edu/garson/dye/docs/tafthart.htm.

SUGGESTED SIMULATION SCHEDULING

SIMULATION FORMAT A
USING A PERIOD OF WEEKS WITH SCHEDULED NEGOTIATING (CLASS) PERIODS

1. First Class Meeting - *Simulation Introduction*

   a. Instructor introduces simulation. Overall objectives are explained.
   b. Participants are assigned to teams and introduced to their counterparts.
   c. Rules of the simulation are discussed and clarified. Additional rules and modifications desired by the instructor are announced.
   d. Schedule, room assignments, and purposes of future meetings are outlined. Deadline for negotiating a contract is specified, and scope and nature of the final evaluation session are determined.
   e. Students should study all *Labor Agreement Negotiations* materials. The authors have found that Fisher & Ury's book, *Getting To Yes*, is an excellent supplement in assisting students' preparation for this simulation. *(For a summary, see the following website: http://www.colorado.edu/conflict/peace/example/fish7513.htm)*. Teams are dispersed to private meetings to organize, specify roles, assign duties, etc. Each team should decide whether it wishes to meet privately before the next class period for additional planning and data collection.

2. Second Class Meeting - *Team Planning*

   Teams meet separately to:
   a. Decide on roles if they have not previously done so.
   b. Analyze materials in simulation package.
   c. Discuss the problems to be negotiated.
   d. Prepare for a successful negotiation. Students need to develop a mental image of what they want from these negotiations. Form 1, the *Negotiation Preparation Plan* found on page 10, gives students a starting point for developing their team's plan of action.
   e. Develop specific bargaining proposals and identify source materials pertinent to each. Roughly state interests, proposals, and counterproposals. Each team should use a form, such as Form 2 found on page 11, to list its initial proposals in a way that can be communicated clearly to the other team.

4

3. Third Class Meeting - *Opening Bargaining Session*

    a. Chief negotiator for each team serves as its facilitator, sets order of team presentations, and introduces team members.
    b. Each team's proposals are presented to opponents (use Forms 2 and 3) with brief supportive arguments.
    c. Teams meet separately to:
        • React to counterpart's initial proposals.
        • Discuss weaknesses in own and counterpart's proposals.
        • Determine and rank importance of counterpart's and proposals.
        • Pinpoint major and minor differences in proposals; select areas of overlap where "win-win," accommodation, or compromise is possible.
        • Determine costs of various proposals, where possible.
        • Plan strategy arguments regarding positions, compromises, or tradeoffs.
    d. Serious bargaining by teams commences as time permits.

4. Additional Negotiation Sessions (as determined by instructor)

    a. Teams continue to bargain over issues and proposals. Proposals and counterproposals may be recorded for future reference by using Form 4 (see page 12). Each team is responsible for maintaining a log that lists all points of agreement.
    b. Throughout the bargaining, each team may caucus when members are not sure how to react to a counterpart's proposal or demand. Caucus time generally should not exceed 15 minutes unless mutually agreed upon.
    c. If a bargaining impasse is reached, or if either team feels the other is not bargaining in good faith, they may ask the instructor to act as mediator.
    d. Negotiations are concluded with agreement on a new contract, or a strike by the union.

5. Final Class Meeting(s) - *Review and Evaluation*

    a. Each union and management team presents their summary reports highlighting significant contract changes and other results of their negotiations.
    b. Teams may discuss the concessions they would have been willing to make; the snags they ran into; the additional preparation that would have been helpful; the strengths and weaknesses of their presentations and bargaining techniques/strategies; and the degree of their own personal and emotional involvement in the simulation.
    c. The instructor may provide additional opportunities for individuals and teams to evaluate this learning experience.

SIMULATION FORMAT B
USING A CONCENTRATED SCHEDULE

The two concentrated simulation schedules provided here include the same general steps outlined in Simulation Format A but have a more intensive bargaining schedule. These schedules are particularly useful for continuing education classes or training seminars and may be adapted as appropriate. **Students must have reviewed the *Labor Agreement Negotiations* materials prior to the first meeting.** The authors have found that Fisher & Ury's *Getting To Yes* is an excellent supplement for this simulation.

1. **Weekend/ Two Day Format**

   a. Saturday 9:00 A.M. to noon
   Simulation introduction and team planning (same as Steps #1 and #2 for Simulation Format A).

   b. Saturday 1:00 P.M. to dismissal and Sunday, 9:00 A.M. to 1:00 P.M. (deadline)
   Opening and continuing negotiation sessions (same as Steps #3 and #4 for Simulation Format A).

   c. Sunday, 1:00 P.M. to dismissal
   Review and evaluation session (same as Step #5 for Simulation Format A).

2. **Weeknight/ Accelerated Format**

   a. Evening 1, 7:00 P.M. – 10:00 P.M.
   Simulation introduction and team planning (same as Steps #1, #2, #3a,b for Simulation Format A). *Conclude with the Opening Bargaining Session and/or exchange of proposals.*

   b. Evenings 2 - 3, 7:00 P.M. – 10:00 P.M.
   Continuing negotiation sessions (same as Steps #3c,d and #4 for Simulation Format A). *Suggested contract deadline 8 P.M., Evening 3.*

   c. Evening 3, 7:00 P.M. – 10:00 P.M.
   Continue negotiation sessions depending on established deadline.
   Review and evaluation session (same as Step #5 for Simulation Format A).

PARTICIPANT ROLES

The *Labor Agreement Negotiations* simulation can be adjusted to various team sizes and time and space limitations. As a rule, the optimal arrangement is three to five members per negotiating team. The suggested roles provided here are intended for five-person teams. The teams themselves must determine who will assume each role and the scope of each member's duties and responsibilities during the simulation. If more than five persons are assigned to a team, the extra person or persons can assume additional roles and duties that the team believes will be helpful. One role could be as observer or team historian. This role allows an individual to create a "learning history" of the team's negotiation experience.

SUGGESTED COMPANY AND UNION ROLES

Company

1. **President of company**--serves as chief negotiator for team.
2. **Vice president of human resources**--provides information relating to wages and benefits; works in liaison with controller; performs research on employment issues as deemed important by the team.
3. **Controller (company treasurer)**--works with vice president of human resources to supply data related to costs incurred by company for various proposals.
4. **Administrative assistant to president**--compiles information received from vice president of human resources and controller and assists president in formulating arguments and counterproposals.
5. **Director of manufacturing operations (St. Louis plant)** – works to ensure customer needs are met and that productivity issues are addressed.

Union

1. **Union business representative**--serves as chief negotiator for team; provides supportive data and proposals and counterproposals to company as appropriate.
2. **Local union president**--supplies union business representative with demands of bargaining unit and emphasizes priorities of employees.
3. **Local union secretary-treasurer**--collaborates with local union president to establish priorities for employee demands; assists in providing union business representative with data and information at variance with company proposals.
4. **Chairperson of the grievance committee**--provides insights about employee complaints about company policies, supervision, and working conditions; works with team members to solidify bargaining strategy.
5. **Chief steward** – provides information about work/life issues that impact union membership

BASIC RULES

1. Consultation with or among the other team(s) or with individuals on the other team(s) prior to or during the course of the simulation is prohibited, unless permitted by the instructor and by mutual request of both sides. This rule includes sharing of research information and discussion of issues, demands, positions, and strategies.

2. Both teams may use considerable ingenuity and imagination to develop their proposals and counterproposals; however, proposals that are not logically derived from the materials or from the contract are not permitted. Participants are encouraged to study the current contract in depth and assertively pursue their interests.

3. Teams may do additional research to find information (economic data, wage and benefit data, or other contracts) to support their interests. Here, too, any research findings used in the simulation must be logically applicable and must not attempt to alter the materials or issues as presented in *Labor Agreement Negotiations*.

4. The instructor sets the deadline. Normally the deadline will not be extended. A new contract must be agreed upon by the deadline, or a strike will occur. The parties should not negotiate under the assumption that the strike deadline will be extended.

SUGGESTED FORMS FOR USE DURING SIMULATION

FORM 1: NEGOTIATION PREPARATION PLAN

FORM 2: INITIAL BARGAINING PROPOSALS

FORM 3: PROPOSALS FOR OPENING BARGAINING SESSION

FORM 4: SEQUENTIAL PROPOSALS AND COUNTERPROPOSALS

FORM 1: NEGOTIATION PREPARATION PLAN

Negotiating Team	My team	Counterpart team
Interests List in order of importance. Interests define the problem, so focus on party's needs, concerns, fears, instead of on positions.	• • • •	• • • •
BATNA (Best Alternative To a Negotiated Agreement) What will you do if you do not reach agreement? Generating a BATNA requires you to: (1) create a list of actions you might take if no agreement is reached (e.g., strike, ask for a mediator); (2) convert some of them into practical alternatives (take a vote of membership to authorize a strike); and (3) select the one alternative that seems best.		
Reservation Point This is the worst you are willing to accept and still agree to the contract.		
Target/ Goals What do you want?		

For an agreement to be viable, it must meet the following criteria:

1. Meet the key interests of both parties.
2. Agreement proposed must be *at least* as good as BATNAs/ meets the reservation points.
3. Must align with the facts and data available.

Possible Solution(s):

Adapted from Hildy Teegen, George Washington University.

FORM 2: INITIAL BARGAINING PROPOSALS

Proposal	Estimated Cost (per hour or per year)	Current Contract Article	Comments

F0RM 3: PROPOSALS FOR OPENING BARGAINING SESSION

Proposal	Team Position and Brief Supportive Statement
1.	
2.	
3.	
4.	
5.	
6.	
7.	
8.	
9.	
10.	
11.	
12.	

FORM 4: SEQUENTIAL PROPOSALS AND COUNTERPROPOSALS

Proposal	Comments

 # THE COMPANY

History

Midwest Plastics Company, Inc., is a privately owned corporation with headquarters in St. Louis, Missouri. The company in mid-2003 operates two manufacturing plants. The St. Louis plant produces plastic injection molding products. The second, smaller non-unionized facility, located in a small town outside of Harrisonville, Missouri (about 40 miles southeast of Kansas City, Missouri), also produces plastics extrusions. Each plant has a director of manufacturing operations. Negotiations are under way at this time with the St. Louis union.

Most of the St. Louis plant's products are sold regionally to major manufacturers and other nearby firms that require customized plastic components. Examples include housings and parts for items such as communications equipment, utensils, computers, games, containers, appliances, and tools. In addition, the St. Louis plant has secured a number of large customized orders from defense and other contractors during the past several years. The firm's sales engineers design molds according to each customer's specifications. When these molds are not in production, sufficient storage space exists to store them at the plant.

Owen Edwards, former chairman, founded Midwest Plastics in 1955. In 1964, he built a new plant in St. Louis to replace his first plant and to accommodate the growing business. Management philosophy and staff behavior at that time were very authoritarian, and employees became dissatisfied with a number of the company's rather strict and arbitrary policies and rules. Employee problems magnified as the firm grew in size, and an employee, who had formerly been associated with the union in another plastics firm, initiated a union-organizing effort. In 1965, the Federated Chemical and Plastic Workers Union became the exclusive bargaining agent for the St. Louis plant employees after a short but hostile campaign and election.

Because many plastics products are lightweight but bulky, shipping costs are often a large percentage of delivered selling price. In order to reduce shipping costs while reaching new regional markets, Edwards purchased the second plant in Harrisonville, Missouri, in 1973. In 1975, Edwards stepped aside as president and turned the reins over to Patrick Kelly. Kelly started working for the company while still in college, and he was successively promoted over the years. His thorough knowledge of all aspects of the company's operations assisted him immeasurably in stabilizing company operations. A competent and supportive managerial staff had been developed under his leadership.

Management

The company's 11-member board of directors currently consists of Patrick Kelly, the company treasurer, the directors of manufacturing operations from the St. Louis and Harrisonville area plants, the vice-president of sales, two investment bankers, and four descendants of Owen Edwards. When Owen Edwards died in 1992, his youngest daughter,

Lorene Simmons replaced him as board chair. Lorene's years as chair, at best, were marked by constant intra-family power struggles. In 1996, Tom Davis, a CPA and investment banker, replaced her as board chair.

Owen Edwards' older son, John, and two older daughters, Jan and Pam, had removed themselves from direct involvement in the company during their father's lifetime. At the time, of Owen Edwards' death in 1992, the company's board of directors was expanded so that each of his children or their descendants would have a seat on the board. The four family board members are Lorene Simmons, her son, Rick, and John's two children, Barry and Larry Edwards. Rick, Barry and Larry are active in the day-to-day management of the company. Rick is involved in sales and Barry's twin brother, Larry, is an engineer and has expressed his dislike for upper-level management responsibility. There is intense rivalry between the three grandsons. Often, they disagree just for the sake of disagreeing.

Upon Kelly's retirement in September 2002, Barry Edwards, grandson of the founder, became president. He had been with the company for three of his thirty-seven years. Barry Edwards is proud of his smooth, sophisticated style of management. He feels that he has the fresh, modern management approach that Midwest Plastics needs in dealing with the problems of the future. His rivals feel that Barry has more style than substance. Barry Edwards and board chair, Tom Davis, get along fairly well. Prior to joining Midwest Plastics, Barry had been a vice president of planning and customer services for a large food service company. Barry lacks hands-on manufacturing experience. To compensate, he has spent a great deal of time learning from his front-line operations people. This will be Barry Edwards' first labor contract negotiations session. Faced with an economy that has been mired in a recession, the board expects Barry Edwards to continue to look for growth opportunities. The board had become accustomed to annual sales growth accompanied by profit growth of three percent or more per year. The board's mandate to Barry Edwards is clear - *increase sales, reduce costs to the industry average and increase return on assets to a level equal to the industry average.* He hopes to return annual sales growth to the five to ten percent range over the next three years.

Manufacturing Improvements

Early in 1977, automated equipment was introduced in the St. Louis plant. Approximately one million dollars' worth of equipment and machinery was purchased over the next three years. The purchase of new equipment and machinery made possible a reduction in the number of plant employees; by 1985, the St. Louis plant bargaining unit was approximately half the size it was in 1977. However, the size of the bargaining unit has remained relatively stable during subsequent years. Generally, the company employs two shifts, which operate five days a week. Since business is frequently slow in the summer, layoffs have been commonplace during those months. At other times orders are heavy, and weekend overtime has extended over a period of several months.

Concurrent with the present contract negotiations, company management is considering several options to improve its competitive position. In the past decade, Midwest Plastics has faced increased pressures from foreign competition, primarily manufacturers from Japan, Korea, and Taiwan. Manufacturers in Southern U. S. and other so-called "right-to-work" states have penetrated markets once considered secure by the St. Louis plant. Other competitors may build plants in Mexico under the North American Free Trade Agreement (NAFTA). Due to these competitive pressures, the company is considering whether to invest additional millions of dollars in automated machinery at the St. Louis plant, expand facilities at the Harrisonville plant, or possibly close both Missouri plants and move all manufacturing operations elsewhere.

During the 1990s, Midwest Plastics achieved moderate operating profits due to favorable economic conditions and the demand for its products and services. However, as of 2002, approximately 55 percent of this profit came from operations at the smaller Harrisonville plant. Wage rates at this second plant were about 10-20 percent lower than those at the St. Louis plant. Current financial statements for the St. Louis division can be found on pages 48 and 49.

In mid-2003, economic conditions facing the company are mixed. Although general demand for company products appears favorable, uncertainties surrounding the U.S. and world economy and the long-term prospects for the defense industry are among the company's major concerns. It is anticipated that several customers are expected, as a condition of continuing to do business with Midwest Plastics, to demand substantial product cost reductions along with guaranteed quality and delivery times. Based on industry trends, it is expected that Midwest's major customer will demand that the company conduct new product research and development and bear those costs as a condition of doing business with them.

Company management feels that acquisition of new plant and equipment would give it the production capacity needed to handle several million dollars' worth of additional business annually. The union is aware of these possibilities and is quite concerned about a possible phase-out or shutdown of the St. Louis plant. On the other hand, the company is currently faced with the imminent probability of receiving several major orders from a number of firms including a local defense contractor. Because of the company's present production capacity limits at its two plants, these orders would be extremely difficult to fill if a strike occurred at the St. Louis plant. The union is aware of these pressures on company management.

 THE UNION

History

Local No. 1243 of the Federated Chemical and Plastic Workers of America, AFL-CIO, was certified as the exclusive bargaining agent for Midwest Plastics plant employees in St. Louis in 1965. The "parent" union represents other workers in the St. Louis metropolitan area, and the union business representative associated with Midwest's employees handles union affairs for several other union locals established at other firms. There are currently 88 employees in the bargaining unit.

When the St. Louis plant was organized, employees felt that company management was insensitive to their needs and interests. Requests for wage increases and improved working conditions were routinely ignored or denied. Organizational efforts by the union received enthusiastic support from most of the production and maintenance workers, and the union won the election by an overwhelming majority.

The former union business representative (or business agent), Roger Brunner, had been chief negotiator for Midwest employees during negotiations for some 20 years. In these negotiations, Brunner had numerous difficulties in working with his own union bargaining committee. This was due primarily to the changing composition of the plant work force and the bargaining committee, and Brunner's problems in communicating with the employees. As a result of these factors, employees voted to strike rather than to accept the terms of a new contract as first offered them in both 1980 and 1983.

During the 1980 five-week strike, the company hired a number of replacement employees. The final settlement produced rather insignificant gains to the employees over those provided in the rejected contract offer. Further, the company hastened its automation process, and about half of the employees in the bargaining unit prior to 1980 were laid off permanently. There was a three-day strike in 1983 over a cost-of-living (COLA) wage dispute. The company refused to grant the union's demands on this issue, and the union ultimately "caved in." There was no strike in 1987, but there was a lingering resentment among a large segment of the rank and file toward the union's 1987 negotiating results.

In January 1990, Roger Brunner abruptly announced his retirement as business representative for Local 1243, just six months before the current contract was to expire. In an attempt to find his successor, several union employees were considered, but the final choice for this position was Doris Campbell. Campbell had attained a B.A. degree in political science and labor economics in 1975 from a small Midwestern liberal arts college. She decided to pursue a career in the labor movement, beginning with several administrative positions with the AFL-CIO in Washington, D.C. She then accepted a position with the Federated Chemical and Plastic Workers of America as a field organizer and staff assistant working out of the union's division office in Chicago. When Roger Brunner retired, Campbell applied for his position; she eventually was appointed as union business representative, assuming all of Brunner's previous area and contract responsibilities. Campbell is now 50 years old.

Doris Campbell moved to St. Louis and served as chief negotiator for the union in the 1990, 1993, 1996 and 1999-2000 negotiations. At first, she relied heavily upon local union leadership. In 1993 and 1996, she was able to negotiate a first year signing bonus and wage increases for the second and third years of a three-year contract. However, company management refused to budge on most union proposals. The union membership narrowly approved the 1996-1999 agreement, but members were quite outspoken concerning their dissatisfaction with the limited improvements.

Negotiation Difficulties

The last round of negotiations in 1999-2000 was contentious. There were threats of a strike by the union. The company countered by threatening to move a substantial amount of the work to the non-union Harrisonville-area facility. The parties agreed to extend the contract for about a year, and agreement was finally reached with the assistance of a Federal Mediation and Conciliation Service (FMCS) mediator. The final agreement was ratified by the slimmest of margins in early July 2000. The current contract expires on July 31, 2003.

Two of the union leaders who served on the 1999-2000 contract bargaining committee are members of the present union bargaining team. Both of them, the union secretary-treasurer and the grievance committee chairperson, voted to reject the contract offered in 2000. The new president of the local, Oscar Belmont, was elected to office in 2001 using a campaign that emphasized that the previous local union president, Allen Eberhardt, had been "too cozy" with management. Belmont is a lead person in the plant, and he has vowed that it is the "union's turn" to make significant gains in contract negotiations.

Current Threats to Union Security

Doris Campbell believes that the current negotiations are crucial to her role as a business representative as well as to the local union. She is tacitly concerned that the company could threaten to close the St. Louis plant and transfer production operations to its second (Harrisonville-area) plant, or to a new plant where labor costs might be lower. However, she does not believe that such a move would be practical or economically possible for the company at this time because of its present and projected production requirements, and the need to be close to the customer. Further, the economy has been "mixed" and there were reports of expansion in the service sector. As a realist, Campbell is aware that increased factory closings and layoffs have led to a rather "soft" labor market with local unemployment rates being significantly higher than in previous years.

Campbell, while tenacious, has a soft-spoken, even-handed demeanor that is quite in contrast to that of Roger Brunner, who was known for his temper and rather "gruff" vocabulary. In a pre-negotiation conference with new company president Barry Edwards, Campbell indicated that non-economic issues were presently just as serious as economic ones. She pointed out that various problems in the plant were making employees "prepared to strike." The national union office had authorized a strike fund allotment to Local 1243 for weekly payments to union members in the event of a strike. Campbell insinuated that the national union strike fund was more than adequately endowed, but she would not reveal the total amount of this fund. She told Edwards that the union members could definitely "hold out as long as necessary" to get a fair contract in this year's negotiation sessions. Campbell also reminded Barry Edwards that there had been several strikes by employees of other companies over issues similar to those at Midwest. She said that she could not predict whether Midwest's employees would do likewise in order to pressure management to agree to certain union proposals.

Campbell has informed union members that a "tough negotiating round" was likely, as economic conditions have changed substantially from previous years. Campbell and the other members of the union bargaining team must legitimately present all issues suggested by the rank and file as justifiable demands for discussion and consideration at the bargaining table. However, as negotiations continue, the union team must be able to signal to the management side those proposals that are less important to the acceptance of a final contract. In the past, negotiators sometimes accomplished this by showing a lack of enthusiasm in making certain demands, by failing to return to a demand or proposal as negotiations progressed, or by withdrawing a number of demands during negotiations as a matter of compromise. During the 1999-2000 negotiations, this was handled mostly by Doris Campbell, but with considerable difficulty. At times, her judgment concerning the logic and practicality of the union's demands conflicted with the desires of certain employees, including members of the union bargaining team.

An Uncertain Future

Doris Campbell realizes that the company probably will reject the wage and benefit increases and other improvements that her bargaining committee wants. Through her education and experience, she is acutely aware that recent years have been troubled times for many blue collar labor unions. With union membership in many manufacturing firms declining, Campbell feels that the union should be cautious in pushing for wage rates that would be significantly higher than those paid by Midwest's competition. Some unions have been forced to accept wage freezes, and even wage and benefit cuts, because of economic and competitive factors.

At the same time, Campbell believes that current wage rates paid to union employees in the St. Louis plant are quite low when compared to other St. Louis area wage rates and in relation to the company's profitability and ability to pay.[3] Campbell and her union members have become quite incensed at reading about extreme increases in pay and bonuses given to U.S. corporate executives by comparison to wage adjustments for workers. In terms of constant dollars, wages have been relatively stagnant for most U.S. workers, and employees at Midwest, too, have seen

---

[3] See Prevailing Entry Wage Rates for Selected Occupations (page 50). According to the Bureau of Labor Statistics (http://stats.bls.gov), in 2000, private sector non-unionized workers received, on average, wages 16 percent lower than their unionized counterparts. Total compensation was approximately 26 percent lower for the non-union employee, in part, due to the greater benefit package granted unionized employees. Many studies have found that union workers are more productive than nonunion workers (see J.T. Addison and B.T. Hirsh, "Union Effects on Productivity, Profits, and Growth: Has the Long Run Arrived?" *Journal of Labor Economics* 7 (1989), pp. 72-105 and D. A. Dilts, E. C. Leonard, and Wayne E. Funk, "Union/Non-Union Quality Differentials: A Case Study of One Manufacturing Firm's Purchasing Experience," *1992 Proceedings of the Midwest Society for Human Resources/ Industrial Relations* (188-195).

little real growth in their incomes even though the company has been profitable. Campbell feels that this year she must "prove herself" by achieving a substantially improved "package" of wages and benefits for Midwest employees. This is her fifth round of negotiations with Midwest Plastics, and she knows she will be held responsible for the results by her membership.

Campbell believes that a mediator from the Federal Mediation and Conciliation Service (FMCS) might be helpful at some stage in negotiations as was the case in 1999-2000, but she would prefer avoiding mediation if possible. Further, she would like to avoid a strike, since she knows that the 1980 and 1983 strikes provided the company with an incentive to reduce employment and speed automation.[4] A strike in 2003 might be an invitation for the company to continue operations by hiring replacement ("scab") workers and attempting to "break" the union.[5] Campbell has carefully studied various union/ management contracts that have been negotiated during the past year and recognizes that the company must gain some concessions and work rule changes to strengthen their competitiveness in an increasingly competitive marketplace. Providing job security for the employees at Midwest Plastics is at the top of her bargaining wish list. Her private thoughts are that "we need a visionary contract that combines and addresses the interlocking needs of our members and the company. We need a win-win for both of us."

---

[4] Although work stoppages impose significant costs on union members, employers and other stakeholders, it is clear from Bureau of Labor Statistics data (http://stats.bls.gov) that strikes and lockouts are the exception rather than the rule in the early part of the twenty-first century. The West Coast dockworkers lockout which shut down loading and unloading at 29 ports for 10 days in late September and early October 2002, created an opportunity for Midwest Plastics. Several companies that had previously done little business with Midwest Plastics, now wanted them to become a preferred vendor as long as they could guarantee supply and price.

[5] When jobs are scarce, replacement workers are more available and perhaps more willing to cross picket lines. Using replacement workers to operate during a strike raises the stakes considerably for strikers who may be permanently replaced. The president of the North Carolina AFL-CIO noted, "Strikes are now a weapon of management. In a lot of cases, management wants you to go out on strike so they can bust the strike and the union" (see Roger D. Staton, "Hiring Replacement Workers: An Insidious Weapon against Labor or Management's Last Bargaining Chip? Labor Law Journal, January 1994; pp. 25-32.). Many strikers are not entitled to reinstatement until there are job openings for which they qualify. Generally, if the strike is over an unfair labor practice, workers who want their jobs back at the end of a strike must be reinstated. Also see www.igc.apc.org/strike for a listing of current strikes in the United States and other major countries.

LABOR RELATIONS AT MIDWEST PLASTICS COMPANY

The company and union bargaining committees have had two pre-negotiation sessions to explore and exchange views concerning major issues over which they expect to bargain. It appears that the current round of formal negotiations will revolve around five issues: *wages, employment security, subcontracting or outsourcing work, work/life concerns, and healthcare benefits.* Although neither side has submitted any formal proposals, the following appear to be the general postures of the parties at the outset of actual negotiations.

Wages

Based upon a recent local wage survey, Midwest Plastics claims that it is currently paying competitive St. Louis industry wage rates for unskilled production employees. The majority of company employees are machine operators making a base wage rate of $10.06 per hour. (See pages 45 and 50 for statistical information for comparative purposes.) Midwest Plastics' employees, however, consider their wages to be totally inadequate. Through their union bargaining committee, they are proposing a $2.00-an-hour wage increase for all job classifications. Employees believe this increase will bring them closer to wages received by most other area workers. Company management considers the normal cost of labor in the plastics business to be approximately 15 to 20 percent of revenues. Paying above this percentage for production workers could place the company in a difficult competitive position. Contracts recently negotiated in local manufacturing firms of comparable size indicate wage increases ranging between 2.5 and 4 percent in the first year. (See page 51 for a summary of local contracts.) The company believes any overall wage settlement at the St. Louis plant should not differ significantly from comparable bargaining agreements. The union states much higher wage adjustments are needed to "catch up" with local wage rates. Also the union is aware that some labor unions have negotiated profit sharing, cost saving, or productivity bonus provisions in their contracts, and the union has suggested this as a possibility for St. Louis plant employees.

Management stated that profit sharing would not be feasible for the St. Louis plant alone, but the union should present a specific proposal if it wishes to discuss some type of bonus provision in return for improved employee productivity and cost savings. Management also mentioned the possibility of another contract signing bonus as an alternative to wage increases during some or over the life of the agreement.

Inequity Wage Adjustments

The company has experienced difficulty in retaining competent maintenance mechanics, who often leave for higher-paying jobs after training by Midwest Plastics. Management would like to increase wage rates of maintenance mechanics. However, in the past, female union employees have complained that the group of men comprising the maintenance mechanic category have unfairly benefited from higher wage differentials than have other plant positions.

The position of group leader requires employees to have extensive specialized training and the added responsibilities of scheduling, operating equipment, and assisting with the training of new employees. The union contends these are tasks normally performed by supervisors and as such wants to define these jobs as "skilled" and achieve a significant wage adjustment for group leaders above the across-the-board wage increases for machine operators.

Seniority Incremental Wage Increases

At the present time, hourly wages are the same for all employees in a particular job classification, regardless of length of service (except for lower starting wage rates for employees with less than one year of service with the company). The union would like to provide an additional incentive for senior employees beyond the across-the-board wage increases. In principle, the company is not opposed to higher increases for employees with several years of service, but is concerned about excessive costs that may result.

Shift Premiums

Shift premiums are paid to employees on the second shift. The union believes that higher shift premiums than presently provided for in the contract should be negotiated. The company feels that all such requests should be considered as part of a total economic package.

Length of Contract

The union is seeking a one or two year contract at this time. Union members believe that the volatile changes in the industry dictate a shorter contract period to improve assessment of trends and the state of the economy. The company would prefer a four-year contract for the sake of stability, better control of costs, and competitive selling advantage.

Cost-of-Living Adjustment

During several negotiations in previous years, the union has advocated a cost-of-living adjustment (COLA), such as a $.01-an-hour increase for each 0.3 increase in the Bureau of Labor Statistics Consumer Price Index, adjusted quarterly. The company soundly rejected these demands, even though some unions have so-called COLA clauses in their contracts. Local union members have instructed the bargaining team to again attempt to attain a cost-of-living provision during these negotiations. Union leadership recognizes that it might have to compromise in other demands to achieve some type of cost-of-living adjustment in the contract. Even with the current low inflation, union officials feel that a COLA clause would be an important wage protection in future years. However, the company is strongly opposed to any COLA formula, believing it to be unrealistic, costly, and outside of its control.

Grievances and Arbitration

The union believes that specific time limits for each of the steps in the grievance procedure should be added to the contract in order to move grievances more rapidly through the procedure. Further, some employees have complained that the company and union have been unwilling to process their grievances all the way to arbitration because of the time and costs involved. The union has suggested the need for an "expedited arbitration" procedure, so as to provide a rapid processing and arbitration of certain types of grievances in an efficient and less expensive way. Although the company believes that these are not needed, management has asked the union to make specific proposals concerning grievance procedure time limits and how an expedited arbitration procedure could be written into the contract.

The union believes the current process for the selection of the arbitrator to be a management tool for not adjudicating grievances expeditiously. During the existing contract period, the company and the union have been unable to agree upon an impartial arbitrator in a timely fashion. The union would like to have the FMCS immediately provide a panel of five (5) arbitrators from which the company and the union would alternately strike names until one remains, who shall then hear the case and make a decision. A coin will be tossed to determine who will strike first. The union wants a clause added to the contract that ensures that the grievance/arbitration process will be completed within seventy-five (75) days of the filing of the grievance. The company believes that the current provision has worked well for almost forty years.

Vacations

The union wants the present vacation schedule expanded to provide additional days of vacation for employees. The company feels that the present vacation schedule in the contract is fair and somewhat above average.

Another issue involves plant wide shutdowns. The union wants to entirely eliminate this section of the current contract, and management wants to modify it. Under the current contract, the company may schedule employee vacations during plant wide shutdowns provided the company notifies employees of this intent by April 1st of each year. During the shutdown period, major plant maintenance work is usually performed. The company feels it has better control when all or most vacations are taken in this manner, since management can schedule work more efficiently and not get caught short on inventories. During the 1983 negotiations, the union agreed to add this provision to the contract, although management maintained that the company always had this right. Ever since, many of Midwest's employees have complained about not having full choice as to when they will take their vacations. Many union workers claim they should be able to take vacations when their family members have their vacations (e.g., school breaks). The union now wishes to delete this section from the contract and allow all employees to choose vacations by a bidding and seniority system.

Although the union feels this section of the contract is too restrictive, the company not only wishes to retain this right but desires to modify the shutdown provision. The company would like to reserve the right to stagger plant wide vacations and to shut down all or any part of the plant for vacation periods as dictated by need. The company feels this arrangement would offer more flexibility to senior employees and spread vacation time over an appropriate number of weeks. The company would then have small groups of employees available to run machines if they were needed.

Holidays

Midwest Plastics' employees presently receive nine paid holidays. The union has suggested that additional paid holidays, such as Presidents' Day, Dr. Martin Luther King's birthday, and the employee's birthday, be added. The company feels that holidays are expensive and that employees don't greatly benefit from holidays. Management believes that the nine holidays provided are adequate, and the company is reluctant to add any more paid holidays.

The union is also concerned about contract language regarding an employee's holiday pay when on layoff. According to the contract, an employee has to work at least seven hours on the scheduled workdays preceding and following the holiday. The union doesn't want anything in the contract that would impose further limitations and feels that there is the possibility of abuse by the company. For example, the company might work an employee up to the day before a holiday and lay him or her off the day of the holiday for a week or so, thus causing the employee to lose holiday pay. Although there have been no specific complaints or incidents of this practice, some union members are concerned about this possibility occurring in the future.

Paid Sick Leave Days

The union wants to increase paid sick leave days from the present four days per year. It claims that most companies now allow about one day of paid sick leave per month. Along with additional paid sick leave days, the union feels that the company should continue to pay eligible employees at the end of the year for any unused days or allow unused sick days to accrue from year to year. The company wants to retain the current provisions and believes a more generous paid sick leave days plan would be expensive and would encourage excessive absenteeism.

The union has also proposed that the eligibility period for paid sick leave days should be changed from two years to the completion of the 45-day probationary period. The company however, believes that paid sick leave days should remain as a benefit for the senior employees. Further, the company wants to specify qualifying dates for the two-year eligibility requirement because it feels the present wording of the sick leave days provision is ambiguous and presents morale problems in terms of fairness. The company believes that employees hired between January 1 and June 30 should be eligible in the second year for sick leave and that those hired from July 1 through December 31 should not be eligible until the following year.

Present company policy can require employees who have been off sick for two or more days to present a note from their doctor when they return to work. The company would like to have this practice put into the contract. There have been instances in which employees obtained a doctor's pad and wrote their own notes. In such cases, the employees were fired. The union, however, objects to the company's policy of requiring a doctor's note. The union claims it is an added and unnecessary expense for an employee to have to go to a doctor for a minor illness and that this company practice shows no faith in an employee's integrity.

Funerals

The union wishes to expand funeral leave provisions to provide additional time off with pay for the death of close relatives such as grandchildren, stepchildren, ex-in-laws, aunts, and uncles. Company policy presently permits employees to take time off without pay to attend funerals of relatives and family members beyond those specifically covered in the contract. They also claim that this policy has been administered inequitably in the past and that some company supervisors are insensitive to requests of employees to attend funerals of relatives and others not specified in the contract.

The union would also like this provision modified to include the following: If a death occurs within an employee's scheduled vacation week, the company will reschedule the vacation week should the employee so desire. The company believes that the existing provision is clear.

Seniority

The probationary period for new employees is currently 45 calendar days. The company would like to have this extended considerably. Supervisors have complained that 45 days are not enough to determine an employee's overall abilities and job performance. During their probationary period, employees do not have recourse to the grievance procedure. The union would like to have this restriction deleted from the contract.

Seniority disputes have been the cause of several internal union conflicts during the past few years. Increasingly, seniority has become the worker's primary guarantee of income security. Whether a worker receives a promotion, is laid off, transferred or put on another shift, these and other aspects of a worker's job responsibilities and earnings depend on seniority.

In one case, a forklift operator/material handler who had been servicing the A line was assigned to the B line. It seems that some of the employees on the B line claimed that the job belonged to them and that she should return to the A line. Company management contended that Article 3, Section 1 gave management the right to direct the workforce.

Life Insurance

An increase in company-paid life insurance benefits from the present $10,000, plus an increase in accidental death benefits, is sought by the union.

Long-term Sickness and Accident Insurance

The company now pays the full cost of sickness and accident insurance for approved absences extending beyond the first week of sickness or accident-related absences from work. This insurance provides weekly benefits of $150.00 per week for 13 weeks for employees with one year's seniority. The union wants to increase these benefits substantially.

Health Care, Dental, and Life Insurance Benefits

The company pays 75 percent of the cost of coverage for health care benefits (medical, hospital, surgical) for participating employees with one year's seniority. Coverage for dependents is offered to those employees willing to pay the additional cost. Specific terms and benefits for this insurance coverage are not included in the labor agreement. The company currently provides these benefits through an HMO. The plan requires a $15 co-pay for physician office visits; hospitalizations are covered at 85% with no maximum. Because employees are restricted to using providers contracted with the HMO, the union considers the current plan to be too restrictive. The union would like the company to provide a plan that includes company payments for dependent coverage, and also allow employees flexibility to use physicians of their choice. The union would like to increase the company's payments to become 85% of all costs of coverage for both eligible employees and their dependents. The company believes that no major changes in health care benefits should be made at this time unless employees are willing to shoulder a larger share of the cost burden.

The union has also suggested that a dental plan would be highly desirable and popular. The union does not know what type of plan would be satisfactory, and it has requested the company to check into this matter. The company response has been non-committal.

The company's medical, hospital, and surgical benefits program conforms with the 1986 COBRA law. However, under present company policy, employees who are laid off are covered for only three consecutive months under the term life insurance program. This layoff coverage is not specified in the contract, nor is it generally known by employees. The union wants the life insurance benefits expanded beyond the present amounts, and the period of layoff coverage lengthened and outlined in the contract.

Other Bargaining Issues

In the past several negotiations, the union has unsuccessfully pressed for a *pension plan*. At a minimum, the company would need to make a $1.00-per-hour contribution per employee in order to participate in a union-sponsored pension plan. The company feels that since the median age of employees is 36, this is not an important issue to them, and it is one the company cannot afford. Alternatively, the union has suggested that the company offer employees a deferred compensation savings program (such as a 401(k) plan) that would include some matching contribution by the company. The company has responded that it would be willing to study this idea, but that such a plan should not be part of the labor-management agreement or part of this year's contractual negotiations.

Both the company and union are dissatisfied with some other seniority provisions in the present contract. The union strongly desires a *formal job-bidding procedure* so employees in lower-skilled jobs could bid on higher-paying jobs with seniority playing a major role in the bidding and selection process. The union feels that most promotions are made on the basis of supervisory favoritism and that management seldom takes employee seniority into account. Although the company is not totally opposed to job bidding, it believes that a formal, plant-wide job bidding procedure written in the contract could cause it to lose flexibility in choosing the most qualified persons for higher-level jobs.

The company is not satisfied with the contractual provision that *layoffs and recalls* be made strictly on the basis of seniority. The company believes that business needs and employee competence should be primary factors in deciding whom to lay off and recall, and management would like to add a contractual clause to cover this issue. The union believes that layoffs and recall should be decided solely by seniority. In addition, the union would like to include the following provision: "Where there is to be a reduction in force (RIF) in the work force which is expected for an extended period (two weeks or more), the union will be given at least three (3) days notice. In addition to the above, the company will adhere to the provisions of the Worker Adjustment and Retraining Notification (WARN) Act."

The company would like to have the ability to hire *temporary workers* during peak production periods. To provide flexibility, meet customer needs, and rapidly fill production requirements, the company would like to have an exempt class of employees (i.e., temporary workers). Because of the requirements of area temporary service firms that bill client companies a placement charge if a temporary worker is hired full-time within the first 60 days, the company wants these employees exempt from union membership during that period of time. The company contends that the better-performing temps may be offered full-time, regular employment as positions become available. At that time, they would become union members. The company contends that the "try before you buy" approach would potentially be beneficial to both the company and the union.

During peak production periods, the company has occasionally subcontracted certain maintenance and specialty work to several outside companies rather than pay additional overtime to Midwest employees or hire additional employees. The Union strongly objects to this practice and wants a contractual clause that would severely *prohibit or restrict subcontracting*. Job security is a critical concern to the employees, and any subcontracting is a major irritant to the union's situation. Company management, however, believes that it must have unlimited freedom to subcontract whenever necessary to promote efficiency and to meet customer requirements.

Because of concerns over possible major reductions or even a permanent shutdown of the St. Louis plant operations, many union members want some form of termination payment or *severance guarantee* for employees added to the contract. Many union contracts provide for a number of weeks or months of wages to be paid employees (usually in relation to their seniority) in the event of permanent layoffs or plant closures. Company management has responded that such employee concerns are speculative and premature, and that any types of termination allowances or payments should be considered only when and if such an event actually occurs.

Part of the female workforce has expressed strong concerns to union leaders that company officials are "behind the times" in meeting their needs. The union has suggested that the company should set up a *day care center* for small children of employees or, alternatively, pay a certain amount to employees for outside day care centers where they could leave their children during working hours. The union has also proposed that a clause should be added to the contract that would grant an employee up to six months of unpaid *family leave* with a guaranteed return to his/her previous job. This would go beyond the requirements of the federal law, the Family and Medical Leave Act. The company views these types of proposals to be costly, of limited or no benefit to other employees, and difficult and inefficient to properly administer. The union has collected information that indicates that U.S. companies are increasingly providing some form of childcare support to their employees. To ease employees' conflicts between work and non-work, the union wants the company to initiate more family-friendly policies such as family leave policies and childcare.

The union has proposed that the term "sexual preference" be added to the non-discrimination provision (Article 5, Section 2). The union also believes that the word "handicap" in this provision should be changed to "disability" to be more inclusive and as defined within the employment requirements of the Americans with Disabilities Act (ADA). The company has not responded to these union proposals. However, the company has proposed that a provision should be added to the contract under which an individual would forfeit all rights under the grievance and arbitration procedure if he or she has filed a grievance alleging discrimination and at the same time has filed a similar discrimination complaint with the Equal Employment Opportunity Commission (EEOC) or some other governmental body.

Within the past several months, three female employees and one African-American employee have complained to the union leadership that they have been *harassed by supervisory personnel* or by other employees. The employees have not filed grievances because of fear of retaliation. The union's business rep, Doris Campbell, is concerned that these actions are not only wrong – they are illegal! The union has requested that the company work collaboratively to develop a "no harassment" policy. So far, management has failed to respond to the union's request. In addition, several union leaders feel strongly that a contract provision is needed to provide a special joint committee through which the union and management could process, investigate, and deal with any such complaint. The company believes that the current grievance procedure, plus legal remedies open to employees (i.e., EEOC), are sufficient and should not be expanded further.

St. Louis frequently experiences summer temperatures of 95 degrees and above. The local union president has requested the office of the Occupational Safety and Health Administration (OSHA) to order the company to close the plant whenever interior summer temperatures are 15-20 degrees or more above the outside temperature, or otherwise to order the company "to *provide cooler working conditions*," a difficult task in the high-ceilinged plant. The union has demanded that the company supply ice water and permit employees to leave their machines at will to obtain fresh water. Until now, the company has observed a strict policy under which employees may not leave their machines unless a foreman or relief person is obtained to maintain continuous production. The company believes that these union tactics and proposals are more harassment than being substantive in nature.

One of the shipping and receiving room employees contended that she cannot work effectively in the warehouse when the outdoor temperature is constantly below 20-degrees F. She has requested that space heaters be placed in the warehouse. The shipping and receiving employees constantly complain that the warehouse is too cold in the winter and too hot during the summer. The company has been unwilling to allocate expenditures to accommodate their concerns.

A number of workers have reported to Oscar Belmont, local union president, that supervisory personnel have told them to "get their act together" because Barry Edwards is considering outsourcing all of the work to the Kansas City-area facility or various non-union shops. Two supervisory personnel, in particular, Tina Tomasloff and Reggie Charles, are alleged to have stated that the president's decision will hinge on the outcome of the forthcoming negotiations.

Several of the union members are still upset because of what they considered to be the "*give-aways*" in 2000. The company gained the right to outsource the janitorial and cleaning tasks to a St. Louis cleaning company. This resulted in the elimination of three positions that in previous contracts were classified as janitors. Some of the more vocal members have contended that this reduction in union membership headcount – while small – will result in the company willing to go-to-the-mat to win greater concessions in the forthcoming negotiations. They contend that this was the company's first step in eliminating various jobs under the guise of increasing productivity. The company believes that this loss was more than compensated for with the addition of two group leader positions on each shift. In the current contract, several job classifications were consolidated. Warehouse personnel (shipping & receiving), material handlers, and forklift operator positions were consolidated into a new material handler job classification. This company demanded this feature to strengthen their competitiveness and flexibility in responding to customer needs. A small contingent of employees have argued that since they worked in 2000 for the same wage rates as in 1999, that the $800 signing bonus that the company gave to each employee was insufficient to compensate for their losses.

One of the younger workers has a brother that worked at the Toyota Motor Manufacturing facility at Princeton, Indiana. After touring that plant with his brother, the Midwest Plastics employee enlisted several other younger workers on the side of employee empowerment. They believe that employees should be empowered to improve their work environment. Broadly defined, they want this to mean that *employees should be involved* in everything including quality, safety, work environment, and various productivity improvements. This group has complained repeatedly that Midwest Plastic's management does not listen to employee suggestions for improvement.

Finally, numerous employees have indicated they would consider taking training and educational courses for job and personal improvement if the company would provide some form of *tuition reimbursement*. Although not a priority item, the union labels this as a contractual benefit of relatively low cost to the company and a positive factor in improving morale and productivity among plant employees.

COMPUTER APPLICATION

Negotiating a labor agreement is a complicated process involving some consideration on almost every factor in a complex array of variables. It is desirable for company and union negotiators to have access to "instant information" concerning the effects of bargaining proposals upon a company's costs, profit margins, and cash flows. In particular, the company side is always concerned about costs that will accrue from any proposal or combination of proposals that are placed on the bargaining table. The union side should have a realistic understanding of such costs, and the union needs data by which it can relate to the company's counterproposals. The computer can be a valuable tool in this process, providing estimates and analysis of changes in bargaining positions on a near-immediate basis.

To facilitate this, a Visual BASIC language computer program has been written. The program may be run as written on any PC with Windows 98 or higher; a copy of Visual BASIC is not necessary. If a negotiating team decides that it would like to utilize this computer program, a representative should request a copy of the program disks that has been provided to the instructor as part of the instructor's manual to accompany this simulation book. It should be emphasized, however, that the negotiations simulation itself was not designed to be programmed on a computer and should not be thought of as a computer simulation. The process of collective bargaining between the parties cannot be adequately experienced just by running a computer program.

Your instructor has also been provided with a computer disk that contains the Collective Bargaining Agreement between Midwest Plastics Company, St. Louis Plant, and Local 1243 of the Federated Chemical and Plastics Workers of America. This may be of assistance in the development of the final contract.

COLLECTIVE BARGAINING AGREEMENT
Midwest Plastics Company, St. Louis Plant, and Local 1243 of the Federated Chemical and Plastic Workers of America

AGREEMENT

THIS AGREEMENT is entered into as of the 1st day of August 2000 by and between MIDWEST PLASTICS CO., INC., located at St. Louis, Missouri (hereinafter referred to as the "Company" or the "Employer"), and Local 1243 of the FEDERATED CHEMICAL AND PLASTIC WORKERS OF AMERICA, AFL-CIO (hereinafter referred to as the "Union").

ARTICLE 1. PURPOSE OF AGREEMENT

Section 1. It is the intention of the parties that this Agreement will establish sound relations between the Company and its employees, which will promote harmony, genuine cooperation and efficiency, to the end that the employees and the Company may mutually benefit; assure a full day's work for a day's pay, and to facilitate peaceful adjustment of differences, which may arise from time to time between the Company and the Union, or between the Company and any employees covered by this Agreement. This Agreement is intended to set forth all the rights of the Union and the employees, all of which arise as a result of this contract.

Section 2. It is further recognized that the interests of its employees are fundamentally the same since the Company must prosper if its employees are to prosper. Therefore, the Company and the Union do hereby mutually pledge themselves to make every effort to make this Agreement the means of improving the relations between the employees covered by this Agreement and the Company, of obtaining fair treatment for all employees of the Company, and improving efficiency so that both may prosper.

- 1 -

ARTICLE 2. RECOGNITION

Section 1. The Company recognizes the Union as the sole and exclusive bargaining agent in the matter of wages, hours of work, and other conditions of employment for all production and maintenance employees at the Company's St. Louis, Missouri facility, excluding office-clerical employees, guards, professional employees, and supervisors, as defined in the National Labor Relations Act, as amended.

Section 2. It is agreed and understood that the above recognition acknowledges and satisfies the representation rights of the Union as the sole and exclusive bargaining agent of the above defined employees to the extent specifically provided by the National Labor Relations Act, as amended. The recognition herein granted to the Union refers only to its right to represent the defined group of company's employees who may be engaged in production and maintenance work at the facility in St. Louis, Missouri, and provided such work is available and the Company determines that said employees should perform such work.

ARTICLE 3. MANAGEMENT FUNCTIONS

Section 1. It is agreed that nothing in this Agreement shall limit the Employer in the exercise of its functions of management, such as, the right to hire new employees, to direct the working force, to promote, layoff, demote, transfer, discipline, suspend or discharge for just cause, to lay off employees because of lack of work, to eliminate jobs, the work to be contracted out, the methods and schedules of production, and the right to set standards of quantity and quality of work, to determine the size of the work force and the location and re-location of its plants. It is agreed that management maintains and retains all of its managerial rights and that they are all vested solely and exclusively in the Employer unless specifically contracted away by this Agreement, and further, that the enumeration of management rights herein shall not be deemed to exclude any other management rights.

Section 2. The Employer will formulate reasonable rules to govern working conditions of the employees and for the regulation of conduct of all employees.

ARTICLE 4. UNION SECURITY

Section 1. It is agreed by the parties hereto that as a condition of continued employment, all persons hereafter employed by the Employer in the unit, which is the subject of this Agreement shall become members of the Union not later than the thirty-first day following the beginning of their employment or the execution date of this Agreement, whichever is the latter.

It is further agreed that continued employment of members in good standing of the Union shall be conditioned upon those persons continuing their payment of periodic dues of the Union. All persons who were in the employ of the Employer prior to the date of this agreement and who are not now members of the Union shall become members of the Union not later than the thirty first day following the execution of this Agreement.

Section 2. The failure of any person to become a member of the Union at such required times shall obligate the Employer, upon written notice from the Union, to forthwith discharge such person. The same shall apply to any person who fails to maintain his Union membership in good standing as required herein.

Section 3. The Company agrees upon receipt of written voluntary authorization of employees to deduct from his first paycheck each month, initiation fees, dues, and such other uniform obligations as are permitted by law owed to the Union.

ARTICLE 5. NON-DISCRIMINATION

Section 1. The Employer shall not intimidate, coerce, discriminate against, interfere with, or restrain any employee by reason of membership in the Union, nor prevent nor hinder any employee from becoming or from continuing to be a member of the Union, nor shall the Employer attempt to encourage membership in another Union.

Section 2. The Employer agrees there shall be no discrimination because of race, creed, sex, age, national origin, color, or handicap.

Section 3. Reference to "he", "him", or "his" in this Agreement shall be taken to include "male" or "female" with no differences or discrimination intended.

ARTICLE 6. REPRESENTATION

Section 1. The processing or investigation of a complaint or grievance shall begin at a time mutually agreed upon by the Union and the Company. The Union shop steward must first obtain permission from his supervisor, or from the plant manager, upon leaving his job.

Section 2. The Union representative shall have the right to confer privately with employees, provided that it is limited to a minimum of time and personnel, and is cleared through the plant manager's office.

Section 3. Grievances, arbitration cases and contract negotiations shall be processed and conducted without lost time to employees. The Union Contract Committee shall consist of three employees.

- 3 -

ARTICLE 7. GRIEVANCE PROCEDURE

Section 1. Any employee desiring to discuss or adjust with the Employer a grievance or misunderstanding involving application or interpretation of this Agreement or matters of hours or working conditions may do so as follows:

Step 1.   Between the immediate supervisor and the aggrieved employee and/or a representative of his choosing.

Step 2.   Between the shop steward and the plant manager or his appointee (if the plant manager is not available), provided the grievance is reduced to writing.

Step 3.   Between the Business Representative of the Union, his committee, and the Employer.

Section 2. Rules governing the processing of the above steps are as follows:

(a)   A grievance shall not proceed to Step 2 unless presented in writing within ten (10) calendar days from date of occurrence or from first reasonable knowledge thereof, whichever occurs first. Once presented, the grievance will be handled expeditiously.

(b)   Provided grievance meetings are held at the convenience of the Company, an aggrieved employee, (or a representative of a group of aggrieved employees), is entitled to be present at any step of the proceedings of his (or their) grievance.

ARTICLE 8. ARBITRATION

Section 1. Disputes and grievances not amicably adjusted through the grievance procedure may be submitted by the aggrieved employee or his representative to an arbitrator for final and binding decision under the rules and in the manner set out below:

(a)   The employee (or his representative) desiring arbitration shall address a written notice to the Employer within thirty (30) days after completion of Step 3 - (Article 7, Section 1) - requesting the parties meet within ten (10) days to agree upon an impartial arbitrator.

(b)   The Employer and the Union shall each select an arbitrator and these two arbitrators shall decide on a third impartial arbitrator within the ten (10) day period. The decision of the arbitrator chosen shall be final.

(c)   If within twenty (20) days from the date of the written notice referred to in (a) herein the parties cannot agree upon an arbitrator, the requesting party shall ask the Federal Mediation and Conciliation Service to submit a list of five persons from which a choice shall be made.

- 4 -

(d)   Said arbitrator's sole function shall be to interpret the meaning of the articles of this contract.

(e)   Except in discharge cases, the Union shall have the burden of proof on all grievances and arbitrations filed by the aggrieved employee or the Union.

(f)   The arbitrator's decision shall be rendered within thirty (30) days of the conclusion of the hearing and shall be final and binding upon both parties. Compliance with the decision shall be handled promptly.

(g)   Expenses of the impartial arbitrator shall be borne equally by the Employer and the Union.

ARTICLE 9. STRIKES AND LOCKOUTS

Section 1. During the life of this Agreement:

(a)   The Company agrees there shall be no lockouts of its employees.

(b)   The Union agrees that there shall be no picketing, supporting strikes, sit-downs, work stoppages or any other activity which interferes with the Employer's operation in the production or sale of its products.

Section 2. If any employee, or group of employees represented by the Union, violates the intent of paragraph (b), the Union shall take immediate affirmative action to prevent such illegal acts and take all necessary steps to the end that work will be properly and orderly resumed. The Union's disapproval of such violation shall be stated in writing to the Employer and such employee or employees involved.

Section 3. Violation of these provisions shall be grounds for discharge without recourse to the grievance or arbitration procedure, although the Company will meet with the Union to discuss an employee's participation, or question, in or regarding the violation of this Article.

- 5 -

ARTICLE 10. SENIORITY

Section 1. Promotional and job security shall prevail in proportion to length of continuous service and ability. Employees promoted or transferred to supervisory or other positions outside of the bargaining unit will have their seniority frozen and will be credited with the seniority accrued if transferred back to the bargaining unit at a future time.

Section 2. In all decreases in working force or recall after layoff, seniority shall govern.

Section 3. Seniority shall be applied on the basis of job classification and length of service of the employee in the particular job.

Section 4. Probationary employees shall consist of all employees employed by the Company for a period of less than forty-five (45) days. This shall include former employees hired as new employees, with loss of seniority. During the probationary period, the Company may, at its discretion, demote, lay off, discipline, suspend, or discharge probationary employees. Neither the Union or the probationary employees have recourse to the grievance procedure.

Section 5. The seniority of an employee shall be broken or terminated if the employee:

(a)   Quits;
(b)   Is discharged for just cause;
(c)   Is absent from work for a period of two (2) consecutive working days without notifying the Company;
(d)   Has been on layoff for a period of more than six (6) months, provided that at the end of three (3) months he has notified the Company and the Union of his desire to remain on the seniority list;
(e)   Is retired or on permanent disability;
(f)   Accepts other employment while actively employed at the Company.

- 6 -

ARTICLE 11. HOURS OF WORK, CONDITIONS OF WORK, AND OVERTIME

Section 1. The work week shall consist of seven (7) consecutive days beginning at 12:01 a.m. Monday and ending at 12:00 midnight the following Sunday night. A work day shall begin at the normal starting time of an employee's shift and shall be the consecutive twenty-four (24) hour period thereafter.

Section 2. Shift schedules shall be:

1st shift: 8:00 a.m. to 4:00 p.m.
2nd shift: 4:00 p.m. to 12:00 Midnight
3rd shift: 12:00 Midnight to 8:00 a.m.

Section 3. Time and one-half shall be paid for all hours worked in excess of eight in any one work day or in excess of forty in any one work week.

Overtime shall be distributed among qualified, eligible employees in an equitable manner.

Section 4. If an employee is sent home due to lack of work within four (4) hours of reporting to work, he shall receive four (4) hours pay. He shall receive eight (8) hours of pay if sent home due to lack of work after four (4) hours.

Section 5. The Company agrees to give employees a ten (10) minute rest period during the first half of each shift and a ten (10) minute rest period during the second half of each shift.

Section 6. Employees are entitled to a thirty (30) minute paid lunch period.

Section 7. Requests for shift changes shall be made in writing to the Company.

Section 8. The need to regularly rotate machine operators and floor persons is recognized by the Company and the Union. This will be accomplished on a three (3) day basis.

- 7 -

ARTICLE 12. <u>WAGES</u>

Section 1. Wages, as used throughout this contract, shall mean and be defined as the hourly wage rate.

Section 2. Payment of wages due shall be made weekly by the Company each Friday for work performed during the previous calendar week.

Section 3. The following wage schedule shall be in effect during the term of this contract, as stated, and shall apply to the job classifications listed in the rates indicated. This listing shall not be deemed to constitute any restriction upon the Company's right to create or discontinue classifications, to assign and reassign work, and to determine the number and abilities of employees required.

WAGE SCHEDULE FOR EMPLOYEES WITH ONE OR MORE YEAR OF SENIORITY

	EFFECTIVE DATE		
JOB CLASSIFICATION	8/1/2000	8/1/2001	8/1/2002
Machine Operator (Production)	9.48	9.76	10.06
Maintenance Mechanic	13.75	14.16	14.59
Assistant Maintenance Mechanic	10.31	10.62	10.94
Material Handler	10.05	10.35	10.65
Group Leader	10.50	10.75	11.00
Truck Driver	12.35	12.70	13.05

Section 4. It is agreed that the wage scale for new hires shall be as follows:
First six months – 80% of job classification wage schedule
After six months – 90% of job classification wage schedule.

Section 5. Employees assigned to the second shift shall receive a premium of fifteen (15¢) cents per hour, and those employees assigned to the third shift shall receive a premium of twenty-four (24¢) cents per hour.

Section 6. Employees with one or more years of seniority on August 1, 2000 will receive a one-time signing bonus of eight hundred dollars ($800.00). Said bonus will be payable to eligible employee on Friday, August 18, 2000, contingent upon ratification of the this agreement by the Union.

-8-

ARTICLE 13. <u>VACATIONS</u>

Section 1. The qualifying date for vacation eligibility shall be June 1 of each year. An employee who has completed one year of continuous service by June 1 of the current calendar year and has worked a minimum of one thousand five hundred (1,500) hours during the preceding calendar year will be eligible for vacation pay on the following basis:

PERIOD OF EMPLOYMENT	VACATION TIME ALLOWED
After one year	5 days
After three years	10 days
After ten years	15 days
After twenty years	20 days

Section 2. The rate of pay for each week of vacation pay will be base rate at the time of vacation.

Section 3. The Company reserves the right to fix plant-wide vacations for or during plant shut-downs, providing the Company posts a vacation shut-down date by April 1 of each year. In lieu of this, employees may request, in writing, preferred vacation dates, no later than thirty (30) days prior to the first day of the employee's requested vacation. Vacation choice, in cases of conflict, is to be made according to seniority within the job classification.

Section 4. Vacations are not cumulative. They are earned and paid on the current year basis.

ARTICLE 14. <u>HOLIDAYS</u>

Section 1. The Company agrees to give each regular employee eight (8) hours pay at his regular straight time rate for the following holidays,

New Year's Eve Day	Fourth of July	Friday after Thanksgiving
New Year's Day	Labor Day	Christmas Eve Day
Memorial Day	Thanksgiving Day	Christmas Day

provided the employee has met the following provisions:

    (a)   The 45-day probationary period has been completed;
    (b)   The employee has worked at least seven hours the scheduled work days preceding and following the holiday;
    (c)   The employee has not refused to work on the holiday if requested by the Company.

Section 2. If a holiday falls during an employee's vacation, the employee, if eligible for the holiday, may receive either an extra day off with pay on a date acceptable to the Company, or an extra day's pay without an additional day off.

- 9 -

Section 3. Holidays falling on a Saturday will be celebrated on the preceding Friday, and when falling on a Sunday will be celebrated on the following Monday. If two successive holidays fall on a Saturday and Sunday, the Company has the option of celebrating them on the preceding Thursday and Friday or the following Monday and Tuesday.

Section 4. All work performed on a holiday shall be paid at twice the regular straight time hourly rate plus the regular holiday allowance.

ARTICLE 15. PAID SICK LEAVE DAYS

Four paid sick leave days each calendar year will be allowed to employees having two or more years of service with the Company. The company will pay eligible employees for any unused sick leave days at the end of each calendar year. Sick leave days may not be taken in conjunction with holidays recognized under this Agreement.

ARTICLE 16. INSURANCE

Section 1. The Company agrees to pay seventy-five per cent (75%) of the cost of medical, hospital, and surgical insurance for each employee who wishes to participate on a voluntary basis. The Company shall notify employees and the Union whenever there are any changes in costs and/or benefits under the insurance plan. The Company will make available similar coverage for dependents of the employee; however, the premium cost for dependency coverage shall be paid by the employee. This coverage will be provided effective August 1, 2000 to all employees with one (1) year seniority.

Section 2. The Company agrees to provide a sickness, disability, and accident insurance program for the life of this Agreement. Weekly benefit payments shall be one hundred fifty dollars ($150.00) per week for thirteen (13) weeks. The Company agrees to pay the full cost of the sickness, disability, and accident insurance program. Employees must have one (1) year of seniority to be eligible for benefits.

Section 3. The Company agrees to provide $10,000 term life insurance to all employees with one (1) year seniority, with an additional $10,000 accidental death benefit.

ARTICLE 17. WAIVER OF BARGAINING

The parties acknowledge that during the negotiation of this Agreement, each has had the unlimited right and opportunity to make demands and proposals with respect to any subject or matter not removed by law from the area of collective bargaining, and that the understandings and agreements arrived at by the parties after the exercise of that right and opportunity are set forth in this Agreement. Therefore, the Company and the Union, for the life of this Agreement, each voluntarily and unqualifiedly, waives the right, and agrees that the other shall not be obliged to bargain collectively with respect to any subject or matter referred to, or covered in this Agreement. When a new problem arises which serves the mutual benefit of both parties, a supplemental agreement may be entered into.

ARTICLE 18. MISCELLANEOUS

Section 1. BULLETIN BOARDS. The Company shall provide the Union with one bulletin board within the plant at a location mutually agreed upon. Bulletins posted shall be limited to notices of meetings and other matters involving the proper business of the Union and shall not contain anything of a controversial, detrimental, or objectionable nature. All postings shall be submitted to and approved by the Company.

Section 2. EXTENDED LEAVES OF ABSENCE. Extended leaves of absence shall be at the discretion of the Company. Requests for such must be in writing to the Company. If granted, when the employee is ready to return, he shall notify the Company in writing. If the leave of absence was granted for sickness, disability, or accident, the employee must be able to present a doctor's statement certifying his ability to return to work. Leaves of absence shall be without pay or penalty, except to the extent that an employee is entitled to payments under the Company's sickness, disability, and accident insurance.

Section 3. FUNERAL LEAVES In the event of the death of a parent, brother, sister, spouse, son, daughter, or present mother-in-law or present father-in-law, the Company will grant a leave of absence from day of death until and including the day of the funeral, not to exceed three (3) days with pay for scheduled working days, provided the employee attends the funeral. In the event of the death of a brother-in-law, sister-in-law, grandparent, grandchild, son-in- law, or daughter-in-law, one day with pay will be given off, that day being the day of the funeral. Evidence concerning attendance at a funeral (such as an obituary notice or statement from the funeral director) and indicating the employee's relationship to the deceased may be required by the Company. Requests for additional time off from work without pay shall be granted or denied at the discretion of the Company.

Requests for time off from work without pay in connection with the death of any person not identified in the preceding paragraph shall be granted or denied at the discretion of the Company.

- 11 -

Section 4. <u>MILITARY SERVICE</u>. The Employer agrees that, upon honorable discharge from military service by an employee who had entered or been drafted in the service of national defense, and upon said employee's request for re-employment within ninety (90) days from the date of honorable discharge, the employee shall be restored to his former position without any loss of seniority. Salary thereafter shall include adjusting increases made to the remainder of the employees during the period of such military service.

Section 5. <u>JURY DUTY</u>. Employees who are subpoenaed and who report for jury service shall receive the difference in pay for the time lost and the amount received as jury pay, but in no case shall the total pay exceed forty (40) hours pay at the employee's regular straight time hourly rate of pay. Jury pay shall not exceed ten (10) working days per calendar year. Proof of jury duty service may be required by the Company.

Section 6. <u>SAFETY COMMITTEE</u>. In order to more effectively promote safety and health, a Safety Committee consisting of an elected member of the bargaining unit from each shift and Company representatives will meet on a regular basis each month. Constructive recommendations, following inspection, investigation, and review of health and safety conditions and practices, or the investigation of accidents, will be made to eliminate unhealthy and unsafe conditions and practices, and to improve existing health and safety conditions and practices.

Section 7. <u>SAVINGS CLAUSE</u>. If at any time during the life of this Agreement, any term or provision contained therein is in conflict with any applicable valid Federal, State, or City law, such term or provision shall continue in effect only to the extent permitted by such law. If any term or provision is or becomes invalid or unenforceable, such validity or unenforceability shall not affect or impair any other term or provision of this Agreement.

ARTICLE 19. <u>DURATION</u>

This Agreement shall become effective and shall continue in full force and effect from the 1st day of August 2000 until the 31st day of July 2003. This Agreement shall be automatically renewed for additional periods of one (1) year each, from year to year, from and after the termination of this Agreement or in any subsequent year for which this Agreement is in force, unless at least sixty (60) days prior to the termination of the original period of this Agreement or any renewal thereof, either the Company or the Union gives the other party written notice of any intention to request alteration, amendment or termination of this Agreement.

- 12 -

Pending negotiation of any proposed amendments, changes, or termination of this Agreement, this Agreement shall remain in effect until a new one is reached or until written notice by registered mail, return receipt requested, has been sent by one party to the other that negotiations have terminated. After the serving of such written notice, there shall be no strike or lockout during the subsequent forty-eight (48) hour period.

IN WITNESS WHEREOF, the parties hereto have executed this Agreement this 1st day of August 2000.

FEDERATED CHEMICAL AND PLASTIC
WORKERS OF AMERICA, AFL-CIO

by _Doris Campbell_   _Allen Eberhardt_

DORIS CAMPBELL, REPRESENTATIVE   ALLEN EBERHARDT, PRESIDENT
FCPWA, AFL-CIO   LOCAL 1243, FCPWA

MIDWEST PLASTICS COMPANY, INC.

by _Patrick Kelly_   _Rebecca Hartman_

PATRICK KELLY, PRESIDENT   REBECCA HARTMAN, VICE
PRESIDENT - HUMAN RESOURCES

- 13 -

STATISTICAL DATA
& OTHER INFORMATION

This information has been developed and shared between the union and management prior to beginning of negotiations

EMPLOYEE DIVERSITY
(Number of employees = 88)

Seniority of Employees

10 years and over	24
7 to 10 years	19
5 to 7 years	11
3 to 5 years	19
1 to 3 years	15
Less than 1 year	--

Average Length of Service

7.6 years

Gender

Male	17
Female	71

Race of Employees

Black	34
White	43
Asian	4
Hispanic*	6
	88

*Note: Some BLS data classifies Hispanic as ethnic distinction rather than race.

Age Categories of Employees (average 36)

Over 50	8
40 to 50	14
30 to 39	48
20 to 29	18
Under 20	0
	88

Ethnic Background

The workforce also includes 8 native Bosnians.

Marital Status

Married	43
Single	45

Average Number of Dependents

1.47
1.87

Extrapolated Seniority Tables Based on Current Employees

	8/1/03	8/1/04	8/1/05	8/1/06
Less than 6 months	0	0	0	0
6 months but less than one year	0	0	0	0
1 year	5	0	0	0
2 years	10	5	0	0
3 years	5	10	5	0
4 years	14	5	10	5
5 years	6	14	5	10
6 years	4	6	14	5
7 years	1	4	6	14
8 years	5	1	4	6
9 years	14	5	1	4
10 years	4	14	5	1
11 years	0	4	14	5
12 years	4	0	4	14
13 years	2	4	0	4
14 years	3	2	4	0
15 years	0	3	2	4
16 years	2	0	3	2
17 years	4	2	0	3
18 years	4	4	2	0
19 or more years	1	5	9	11
	88	88	88	88

Current Employees by Job Classifications

Job	Number	Base Wage Rate* (dollars)
Machine Operators (Production)	66	10.06
Maintenance Mechanics	7	14.59
Assistant Maintenance Mech.	2	10.94
Group Leaders	4	11.00
Material Handlers	7	10.65
Truck Drivers	2	13.05

* Note: At this time, no employees are working at the new hire rate.

FINANCIAL AND WAGE DATA

Wage Cost Table Based on Current Average Wage Rates

Job Classification	No. of Employees	Average Wage Rate*	Individual Daily Wages	Job Classification Daily Wages	Yearly Cost**
Machine Operators	66	$ 10.28	$ 82.84	$5,427.84	$1,411,123.84
Maintenance Mechanics	7	14.72	117.76	824.32	214,323.20
Assistant Maintenance Mechanics	2	11.02	88.16	176.32	45,843.20
Group Leaders	4	11.08	88.64	354.56	92,185.60
Material Handlers	7	10.91	87.28	610.96	158,849.60
Truck Drivers	2	13.15	105.20	210.40	54,704.00
TOTAL	88			$7,603.96	$1,972,029.44

Notes:
*Average wage rates include starting rates, shift differentials, and overtime paid. For 2002: Overall average wage rate per hour = $10. 80; Overall average daily wages paid per employee = $86.41.

**Calculations Assume: Paid hours per employee = 2,080 per year   (40 hours x 52 weeks) and workdays per year = 260 (5 days x 52 weeks).

Approximate Cost Per Year of 1% Increase in Basic Wage Rates

Job Classification	No. of Employees		Hours		1% Wage Increase Per Hour		Year Total
Machine Operators	66	x	2,080	x	$0.103	=	$14,139.84
Maintenance Mechanics	7	x	2,080	x	0.147	=	2,140.32
Asst. Maint. Mechanics	2	x	2,080	x	0.110	=	457.60
Lead Persons	4	x	2,080	x	0.111	=	923.52
Material Handlers	7	x	2,080	x	0.109	=	1,587.04
Truck Drivers	2	x	2,080	x	0.132	=	549.12
TOTAL	88						$19,797.44

Benefit Costs

Dental Plan

A limited dental plan (with an annual deductible and no orthodontics or oral surgery) would cost approximately $23.50 per month per employee. For family coverage, such a plan would cost approximately $74.00 per month per employee.

Sickness, Disability, and Accident Insurance (paid by the company)

Current cost for 13 weeks is $35.00 per month per eligible employee. This entitles each eligible employee to $150.00 per week for 13 weeks if an employee has an extended illness or accident that absents him or her from work beyond two weeks' absence. Each $5.00 per week increment over $150 will cost an additional $3.00 per month per employee.

Life Insurance (paid by the company)

An increase from $10,000 to $15,000 in life insurance would cost approximately $4.00 per month per employee.

Health Care Insurance Benefits (medical, hospital, surgical, and certain "medically necessary prescriptions")

As of January 1, 2003, the cost of the current HMO plan was about $207 per month per employee. The company pays 75% of the cost, and participating employees pay the remaining 25%. Currently, about 40% of the eligible employees are participating in this program.

A "Point of Service" (POS) plan that would allow employees to visit the provider of their choice outside the HMO - (subject to a $350 annual deductible and 20% coinsurance) - would cost an additional $31 per month per participating employee. Under this plan, in each calendar year an insured individual would pay the first $350 of medical expenses; the POS plan would then pay 80% of covered medical expenses thereafter.

Employees who participate in the current HMO plan must pay the premium costs of dependent coverage. These costs are currently $358 per employee per month. Under the POS plan described in the preceding paragraph, dependent costs would be $375 per employee per month. Only a small number of eligible employees have chosen to pay for dependent coverage.

Note: Rapidly rising health care costs are an issue for companies across the country. Premiums are expected to increase significantly. It is reported that Health Maintenance Organizations (HMOs) are expected to charge employers 19 percent more in the St. Louis area for the same health care coverage in 2003. Also see, *News In Review #3* for another perspective on health coverage concerns. Students should consult BNA's Pension & Benefits Reporter and other sources for benefit cost data.

The Union Advantage

Median weekly earnings of full-time union-represented workers in 2001 were about 24% higher as compared to that for non-union workers ($712 vs. $575). The union advantage was even higher percentage-wise for union-represented women, African-Americans, and Hispanics.

Median Weekly Earnings (2001)

	Union	Non-Union	Percentage Differential
Women	$639	$494	29%
African-Americans	$599	$463	29%
Hispanics	$578	$398	45%

Union represented employees also received considerably higher benefits on average than their non-union counterparts.

Source: Median weekly earnings of full-time wage and salary workers by union affiliation and selected characteristics (www.bls.gov).

BALANCE SHEET
Midwest Plastics Company, Inc., St. Louis Division
December 31, 2001 and December 31, 2002

Assets

	December 31 2001	December 31 2002
Current Assets:		
Cash	$ 927,433	$ 842,321
Marketable Securities	470,501	416,498
Accounts Receivable	1,395,879	1,581,612
Merchandise Inventory	2,576,873	3,437,514
Total Current Assets	5,370,686	6,277,514
Property, Plant and Equipment:		
Land	$ 306,130	$ 306,130
Buildings (Net of Accumulated Depreciation)	2,467,508	2,419,258
Equipment (Net of Accumulated Depreciation)	2,019,594	2,202.700
Total Property, Plant and Equipment	4,793,232	4,928.088
Total Assets	$10,163,918	$11,206,033

Liabilities and Stockholders' Equity

Current Liabilities:		
Accounts Payable	$ 1,429,880	$ 1,793,946
Salaries Payable	82,400	84,691
Income Taxes Payable	105,290	90,113
Other Accrued Expenses	36,248	45,879
Total Current Liabilities	1,653,818	2,014,629
Long-Term Liabilities:		
Long-Term Debt	5,057,800	5,080,837
Total Current and Long-Term Liabilities	6,711,618	7,095,466
Stockholders' Equity:		
Capital Stock	765,600	765,600
Retained Earnings	2,686,700	3,344,967
Total Stockholders' Equity	$ 3,452,300	$ 4,110,567
Total Liabilities and Stockholders' Equity	$ 10,163,918	$ 11,206,033

INCOME STATEMENT
Midwest Plastics Company, Inc., St. Louis Division

	2001	2002
Revenues:		
Sales of Merchandise and Engineering Services	$ 11,158,435	$ 10,863,221
Less: Returns and Allowances	211,789	208,388
Total Revenues	$ 10,946,646	$ 10,654,833
Cost of Goods Sold	$ 7,067,334	$ 7,174,291
Gross Profit	$ 3,879,312	$ 3,480,542
Selling and Administration Expenses:		
Salaries Expense	$ 990,520	$ 1,009,942
Depreciation Expense	318,654	315,320
Selling and Administration Expense	517,112	504,388
Total:	$ 1,826,286	$ 1,829,650
Income from Operations:	$ 2,053,026	$ 1,650,892
Other Expenses and Losses:		
Interest Expense	546,242	503,827
Income before Income Tax	$ 1,506,784	$ 1,147,065
Income Tax Expense	501,759	380,540
Net Income	$ 1,005,025	$ 766,525

Notes:

(1) The balance sheet and income statement represent operations in the St. Louis Division only and were prepared primarily for internal management purposes. The company consolidates its financial statements for external reporting.

(2) The company has been unwilling to provide any additional financial information to the union.

Prevailing Entry Wage Rates for Selected Occupations in St. Louis and St. Louis County (2nd Quarter 2002)

Production and Maintenance Occupations	Median Hourly Wage Rate
Assembler, Production	$ 11.33
Drill Press Operator	10.36
Electrician, Maintenance	24.26
Industrial Truck Operator	22.62
Machinist, Journeyman	16.26
Machine Set-Up Operator	11.47
Maintenance Repairer, General	14.20
Mechanic, Maintenance, Factory	14.26
Millwright	19.21
Painter, Spray, Production Line	13.27
Production Machine Operator (Gen. Mfg.)	11.09
Production Machine Operator (Mach. Shop)	11.33
Punch Press Operator	12.43
Sheet Metal Worker, Production	23.45
Tool & Die Maker	22.05
Truck Driver (light)	12.58
Welding Machine Operator	13.43
Woodworking Machine Operator	10.21

Source: 2002 Metropolitan Area Occupational Employment and Wage Estimates, St. Louis, MO-IL MSA. (Bureau of Labor Statistics)

Average Hourly and Weekly Earnings of Manufacturing Workers in U.S.

Current dollars	1990	1995	2000	2001	2002
Average hourly earnings	$ 10.83	12.37	14.37	14.83	15.20
Average weekly earnings	$ 442.00	515.00	598.00	606.00	619.00
Annual % change hrly earnings	--	2.50	3.38	3.20	2.46
Constant dollars (1982 = 100)					
Average hourly earnings	$ 8.29	8.12	8.34	8.37	8.50
Average weekly earnings	$ 338.00	338.00	347.00	342.00	347.00
Annual % change hrly earnings	--	0.40	0.02	0.35	1.57

Source: Bureau of Labor Statistics.

SELECTED EMPLOYMENT PRACTICES
Partial Summary of Selected Comparable Contracts (Second half of 2002)

Union	Boilermakers	International Assn. of Machinists and Aerospace Workers	United Steelworkers	Teamsters Union	Federated Chemical and Plastic Workers
No. of Employees in Bargaining Unit	91	212	102	59	79
Length (Years of Contract)	3	3	3	3	3
Wages: 1st year / 2nd year / 3rd year	$800 signing bonus; no wage increase / $ .50 / $ .50	$ .40 / $ .30 / $ .30	No wage increase; wage reopener provision at end of 15 months	$ .30 / $ .30 / $ .40	2% / 2% / 2%
Average Wage Rate	$13.82	$14.35	$13.49	$15.09	$11.88
New Benefits (compared with previous contract)	Add grandparents and step-parents for funeral leave	New dental plan; new tuition reimbursement plan	Add language to allow change in insurance carriers; same coverage	None	Additional dental plan coverage
Holidays	No change (11 total)	No change (10 total)	No change (9 total)	No change (10 total)	Add Martin Luther King Birthday in 2nd year of contract (10 total)
Vacation	Same: 1-3 yrs. = 1 week; 3-10 yrs. = 2 weeks; 10+ yrs. = 3 weeks	Change 10 years to 8 years = 3 weeks; New: 5 weeks after 20 years	4 weeks after 20 years in third year of contract	No change	No change
Sickness & Accident; Life Insurance	S & A: $165 to $190 for 15 weeks	S & A: from $135 to $165 for 13 weeks	Life insurance from $10,000 to $15,000	Life insurance from $8,000 to $12,000	S & A: Increase from $130 to $175 per week for 20 weeks
Other Benefits Already Provided (Note: Major medical similar to medical, hospital & surgical)	Major medical	Pension plan; major medical	Major medical	Pension plan; major medical	Pension plan; Major medical; Dental plan

St. Louis Region Production, Maintenance & Service Employers (fewer than 500 employees)

Types of Time Off Offered by Companies	Percentage of Companies Offering
Paid Holidays	91%
Unpaid Holidays	17
Holiday Premium Pay	78
Vacation	96
Pay in lieu of vacation	43
Paid sick leave	30
Paid jury duty	70
Time off as a witness	65

Paid Holidays	% of Union Companies	% of Non Union Companies
8 days or less	31.2	26.3
9 days	31.3	28.1
10 days	12.5	30.3
11 days	25.0	7.8
12 or more days	0.0	7.5

Holiday Premium Pay. Of those firms giving holiday premium pay, 78.9 percent paid double time, 10.6 paid time and a half, and 10.5% had other pay arrangements.

MINIMUM AMOUNT OF SERVICE TO EARN VACATION

| Vacation Amount | Years of Service Required | |
	Union Companies	Non Union Companies
One Week	1 yr. or less	1 yr.
Two Weeks	1-3 yrs.	1-5 yrs.
Three Weeks	5-10 yrs.	5-10 yrs.
Four Weeks	10-20 yrs.	10-25 yrs.

Other vacation options. While 43% of companies indicated they paid in lieu of vacation, approximately 11% of employers allow employees to "buy" an extra week of vacation simply by taking time off without pay. (See Brenda Park Sunoo, "Vacations: Going Once, Going Twice, Sold," *Personnel Journal*, August 1996, pp. 72-80.)

ALLOWED (FIXED) PAID SICK LEAVE DAYS PER YEAR

	% of Union Companies	% of Non Union Companies
Under 5 days	18.8	40.8
6-9 days	11.4	14.5
10 days	6.3	3.8
11 days or more	6.0	5.0
No formal plan	6.3	11.6
Don't specifically pay for sick days*	57.2	29.3

The amount of sick leave is often tied to length of service, e.g., an employee may accumulate 2 sick days every three months of service. Historically, many companies had policies that declared that sick days disappeared at the end of the year (rather than allow them to accumulate). This "use them or lose them" mentality contributed to greater absenteeism. To counter this, some organizations allow sick days to accumulate, then pay employees for the number of sick days when they retire or resign.

*Increasingly, organizations are bundling paid vacation, holidays, sick leave and personal days, and allow employees to chose how they use the time off with pay. They may chose to use these days for any purpose. This process allows individuals to tailor-make a portion of the benefit program to fit their needs. Typically, time not used may be allowed to accumulate or employees may chose to take pay in lieu of the time off with pay.

UNUSED SICK DAYS ARE:

	% of Union Companies	% of Non Union Companies
Cancelled	16.7	29.2
Paid for	--	14.3
Carried over	83.3	56.5

Impact of Benefits on Productivity

According to author Wayne Cascio, "Generally speaking, employee benefits do not enhance productivity. Their major impact is on attraction and retention (although there is little research on this issue) and on improving the quality of life for employees and their dependents. … The challenge for executives will be to maintain control over the cost of benefits while providing genuine value to employees in benefits offered" (Wayne F. Cascio, *Managing Human Resources: Productivity, Quality of Work Life, Profits*, 6th edition, Boston: McGraw-Hill, 2003, p. 490).

Sources: Selected Employment Practices data was extrapolated from the results of a Bureau of Labor Statistics survey of incidence and provisions of employee benefits plans, and from proprietary information secured from a St. Louis area industry. The BLS data is based on surveys of firms with 100 or more employees and the other data is based on a random survey of firms employing fewer than 500 employees.

MISCELLANEOUS DATA

CONSUMER PRICE INDEX (C.P.I.) AND INFLATION RATES
U.S. City Average

	Average Annual C.P.I. (all items) (1982-84 = 100)	Annual Inflation Rate (% change in C.P.I.)
1994	148.2	2.5%
1995	152.4	2.9
1996	156.9	3.0
1997	160.5	2.3
1998	163.8	1.6
2000	172.2	3.4
2001	177.1	2.9
2002	178.9	1.3

Source: Consumer Price Index – all urban consumers (www.bls.gov).

INDEXES OF MANUFACTURING PRODUCTIVITY GROWTH AND REAL WAGES (1991 – 2002)
1992 = 100

Year	B.L.S. Index of Productivity	B.L.S. Index of Real Wages
1991	95.1	98.7
1992	100.0	100.0
1993	101.9	100.2
1994	105.0	101.0
1995	109.0	100.6
1996	112.8	99.4
1997	117.6	99.1
1998	124.0	103.0
1999	129.6	104.9
2000	137.5	108.6
2001	139.0	113.4
2002	143.8	114.9

Source: Output Per Hour Manufacturing and Real Hourly Compensation Manufacturing (www.bls.gov).

OUTPUT PER PERSON MANUFACTURING INDEX
(1992 = 100)

Year	Index
1991	93.8
1992	100.0
1993	103.2
1994	107.3
1995	110.7
1996	114.5
1997	120.2
1998	125.5
1999	132.1
2000	139.1
2001	138.8
2002	143.7

Source: Output Per Person Manufacturing (www.bls.gov).

Employees on Layoff and Hiring Projections For Manufacturing Companies in the U. S. (Based upon a quarterly survey conducted by BNA, Inc.)

Employees on Layoff

Percent of companies in manufacturing reporting some employees on layoff status

Date	Percent
July 1995	13%
July 1996	14%
July 1997	11%
July 1998	11%
July 1999	11%
July 2000	8.5%
July 2001	12%
July 2002	16%

Hiring Projections

Percent of companies in manufacturing anticipating an increase in hiring

Date	Percent
July 1995	20%
July 1996	18%
July 1997	19%
July 1998	22%
July 1999	21%
July 2000	25%
July 2001	19%
July 2002	12%

Source: Bureau of National Affairs, Inc., Washington, D.C. (http://www.bna.com/press/2002/worksurv1.htm).

U.S. Unemployment Rates (%) in Manufacturing Industries (in July)

	1995	1996	1997	1998	1999	2000	2001	2002
Manufacturing	5.3	4.8	4.4	4.5	3.8	3.8	5.5	6.7

Source: Unemployment Level Manufacturing Wage and Salary Workers (www.bls.gov).

Manufacturing Turnover*

Median separation rates (excluding layoffs, reductions-in-force, and departures of temporary staff) averaged 1.1 percent of employers' workforces per month in 2001, down from the 1.3 percent in 2000. After climbing to their highest rates in two decades during the late 1990s, turnover rates have declined substantially.

Source: "Weak Economy Brings Sharp Decline in Employee Turnover," BNA News Release (March 14, 2002) (www.bna.com/press/2002/worksurv2.htm).

NEWS IN REVIEW

1: Runaway CEO Pay: The AFL-CIO View

According to Business Week, the average CEO of a major U.S. corporation made 42 times the pay of the typical American factory worker in 1980. By 1990, that ratio had more than doubled to 85 time the factory worker's average wage, and almost quintupled again to a staggering 419 times more in 1998. In 2002, the compensation of top management relative to average compensation of company employees is 475 to 1. In Switzerland, that ratio is 14 to 1. Yet in terms of education and qualifications of the people at the top of those Swiss firms is not much different from that of their American counterparts.

Source: American Federation of Labor-Congress of Industrial Organizations (AFL-CIO), "Executive Pay Watch" (www.afcio.org/paywatch/ceopay.htm).

2: Sluggish Economy Impacts Poverty Level

The U.S. economy grew slowly with mixed results across sectors and regions in late 2002 according to a Federal Reserve Report. In the "beige book" – a report on the country's economic conditions named for the color of its cover – the Fed reported that consumer spending which accounts for more than two-thirds of economic activity was expected to be flat-to-moderate growth for the St. Louis region. Auto dealers noted a drop in sales and the manufacturing sector remained "soft." Fed policy makers cut interest rates by an aggressive half-percentage point to 1.25% on November 6, 2002 in an attempt to jump-start the economy. Current interest rates are the lowest in 41 years.

At the same time, the census bureau was reporting that the poverty rate was rising and household income was falling. Some economists had expected that the poverty rate would continue to rise as unemployment continued rise and the economy remains in a recession. There were 32.9 million Americans living in poverty in 2001. The bureau calculated that for a family of four, the poverty level in 2001 was $18,104. The bureau also calculated that median household income – defined as the point at which half the households earn more and half earn less – declined to $42,228.

Source: Barbara Hagenbaugh and Stephanie Armour, "Several Regions Cite "Sluggish" Economic Conditions," *USA Today* (November 29, 2002), p. 6B; Genaro C. Armas, "Poverty Rises Nationwide as Household Income Falls," *The Associated Press* (September 24, 2002). Also see www.gov for access to various reports of the Federal Reserve.

3: Prognosis: Higher Health Care Costs, Less Care

Americans today are living longer and, in some cases, healthier lives. But that doesn't eliminate the need for good health insurance. Even with the right plan, paying medical bills can be a real headache as health care costs continue to climb. One thing is clear: they are going to pay more and get less.

Medical costs are rising rapidly, and employers are passing more of the expense on to workers for 2003. For many people that will mean increased payments just to be covered by a company health-care plan, along with higher deductibles and bigger co-payments for medical services. And some companies will also seek to save money by cutting back on covered services themselves, pay for supplemental insurance to cover the gap – or do without.

Costs are rising so quickly that many small companies are considering whether they can even continue to offer their workers health insurance, says Larry Boress, vice president of the Midwest Business Group Health, a coalition of employers. Insurers are charging companies with fewer than 25 employees 30% to 40% more to renew their health-care coverage for next year, he says. Larger companies have been able to negotiate increases between 18% and 20%, says Mr. Boress, whose Chicago-based group represents large Midwestern corporations in talks with health insurers.[1]

Employees Pay More

Workers have already begun to shoulder a substantial part of the increasing costs. A national survey of more than 3,000 public and private employers earlier this year by the Henry J. Kaiser Family Foundation, a philanthropic organization based in Menlo Park, California, and the Health Research and Educational Trust, a nonprofit research organization in Chicago, found that employees were paying 27% more on average this year than they did last year for individual coverage by a company health-care plan, and 16% more for family coverage. And those increases in premiums, to an average of $454 for an individual and $2,084 for a family, don't include such out-of-pocket expenses as deductibles and co-payments.

For visits to doctors in the networks of preferred-provider plans, the common most type, deductibles rose 37% to an average of $276, the survey found. For visits to doctors outside the networks, deductibles rose 20% to an average of $488.

The survey respondents also reported a 30% increase in co-payments for brand-name prescription drugs for which generic substitutes were available, to an average of $26, under tiered drug plans, which charge less for brand-name drugs with no substitutes and less again for generic drugs. For the brand-name drugs with no substitutes, co-payments rose 13% to an average of $17, and for generic drugs, co-payments also rose 13%, to an average of $9.

The use of price tiers for prescription drugs has nearly doubled since 2000, the survey found, with 57% of respondents saying their health care plans now use tiering. That's just one of the ways companies are trying to steer employees toward less-expensive health-care options.

Smarter Consumers

The higher costs may drive more companies to consider plans under which the employees get a lump sum to spend on health care. The Internal Revenue Service has ruled that such payments don't constitute income and aren't taxable.[2] Under one variation of this plan, the employer would allot each employee a set amount of money each year for routine medical costs, to be spent largely at the employee's discretion. The goal of these "consumer-driven plans" is to encourage employees to be aware of health-care costs and to shop around. Blaine Bos, a principle of Mercer Human Resources Consulting, says such plans probably won't become widespread until 2004.

Mr. Bos says more companies also are considering so-called scheduled programs, which set the dollar amount they will reimburse for an office visit or procedure, leaving the patient to cover whatever the difference is between that figure and the fee for service. Again, the aim is to encourage people to shop around. Mr. Bos says some union negotiators have resisted such plans, arguing that the employees they represent either aren't prepared to do such sophisticated comparison shopping or are embarrassed to ask about health-care costs upfront.

However companies craft their plans, though, the trend is clear. "With health costs rising so rapidly and no solution on the horizon, workers can expect to pay more and get less coverage," says Drew Altman, president of the Kaiser Foundation.

The Cost of Care[3]

The average annual premium costs by type of plan for covered workers, single, and family plan coverage for 2002 is described in the table below.

TYPE OF PLAN		EMPLOYEE CONTRIBUTION	EMPLOYER CONTRIBUTION	TOTAL
Traditional Indemnity	Single	$ 426	$ 3,156	$ 3,582
	Family	1,630	6,849	8,479
HMO	Single	455	2,309	2,764
	Family	1,960	5,581	7,541
PPO	Single	432	2,687	3,119
	Family	2,152	5,885	8,037
POS	Single	527	2,648	3,175
	Family	2,186	5,987	8,173

Definitions:

HMO (health-maintenance organization): Prepaid medical-service plan in which members must use contracted service providers. The emphasis is on preventive medicine.

PPO (preferred provider organization of hospitals and physicians): Provide for a set fee, services to insurance company clients. Coverage is 100 percent, with a minimal co-payment for each office visit or hospital stay.

POS (point-of-service plan): Allow a choice of receiving services from a participating ("in network") or nonparticipating ("out of network") provider, with only a percentage of out-of-network service costs reimbursed.

Fee-for-service plan: Traditional system where physicians and other providers receive payment based on their fee and insurees are reimbursed according to a set percentage.

Consumer-directed plan: The insured can tap into their health savings account to pay for traditional health services, plus some procedures not covered by traditional plans. Such plans typically have a deductible, as traditional fee-for-service plans do, but the deductible doesn't kick in until the savings account money is used up.

Source: (1) The material contained in this *News in Review* was adapted with permission from Chad Bray, "Prognosis for 2003: Higher Costs, Less Care," *The Wall Street Journal* (November 11, 2002), p. R7. (2) Peter Landers, "Health-Care Costs Are Rising, *The Wall Street Journal* (October 2, 2002), p. D.3. (3) The cost data provided in this Contemporary Issue was adapted from "New Survey Shows Workers are Paying More and Getting Less for Their Health Care Coverage," *Health Research & Educational Trust News* Release (September 5, 2002) and provided here with permission of the Henry J. Kaiser Family Foundation. For additional information the September/October issue of *Health Affairs* (www.healthaffairs.org). The current survey is based on previous surveys conducted since 1991. Visit www.kff.org for archived survey results.

 NEGOTIATION BASICS

Bargaining Systems Differences

Traditional (Adversarial)
- Discredit opponent's position
- Attack individuals
- Present and defend position
- Provide supporting materials
- Continually insist on predetermined bargaining positions
- Negotiate to obtain outcomes for your own best interests
- Use power, pressure, deferral to obtain desired solutions

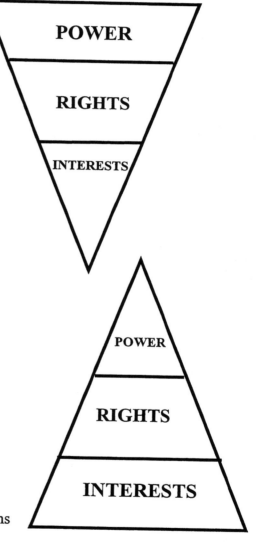

Interest –Based (Non-adversarial)
- Address mutual problems and concerns
- Focus on specific issues – not on individuals or past conflicts
- Explore interests of mutual concerns
- Clearly define mutual interests
- Be open-minded to possibilities and/ or future opportunities
- Satisfy others' interests as well as your own
- Work toward satisfying the interests of all concerned (win-win mentality)
- Define acceptable solutions measured against jointly developed standards
- Use consensus decision making to reach decisions

Source: Adapted from *Interest-Based Bargaining Program* (Washington, D.C.; Federal Mediation and Conciliation Service, 2002). See George Bohlander, Scott Snell, and Arthur Sherman, *Managing Human Resources*, 12th edition (Mason, OH: South-Western College Publishing, 2001) pp. 604–605 for another discussion of nonadversarial bargaining.

Negotiating Styles

Every participant in a negotiation has two important concerns:
1. The concern for substance or outcome of the agreement.
2. The concern with, and the value placed, on the relationship with other parties.

Shortly after the 1962, Cuban missile crisis, then President John F. Kennedy said, "Let us never negotiation out of fear. But let us never fear to negotiate." In a successful negotiation, everyone wins. The objective should be agreement, not victory. While bargaining teams may approach negotiations differently, they should understand the five basic negotiation styles (see Figure below).

The horizontal axis on the Figure indicates degree of cooperativeness, ranging from low to high. A high degree of cooperativeness implies that one desires a long-term harmonious relationship with the other party. Low to high concern for self, or degree of assertiveness, is found on the vertical axis of the Figure. To determine location on this scale, the negotiating team members must ask: "What is *really* important to us?" For example, the union leadership has stated that job security is their top priority. In other words, they will not compromise their need to retain employees' jobs. They will stand firm on this issue.

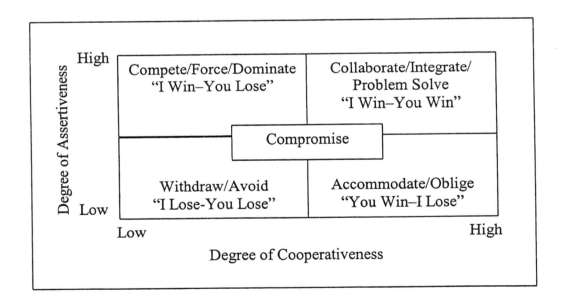

Various combinations of these concerns yield five negotiations styles:

Withdraw/avoid: The withdraw/avoid approach may be appropriate when the issue is perceived to be minor and the costs of solving the problem are greater than the benefits. This tactic is used when one finds it advantageous to hold off or stall, rather than give in immediately to the other sides' requests. This may be an appropriate strategy when time is not important or "to live to fight another day."

Accommodate/oblige: The primary strength of the accommodate/oblige style is that it encourages cooperation. This style is thought of as, "I lose, you win." Because no one wants to lose all the time, this style implies the rule of reciprocity or reciprocity reflex – That is, you give up something now to eventually get something of value in return.

Compromise: The compromise style is called "Win some, lose some." Labor-management negotiations often use compromise. Unfortunately, if you know that the other always compromises, then you will bring inflated (much higher than you expect to gain) demand party brings inflated demands to the bargaining table. As a result, valuable time is wasted trying to identify the real issues.

Compete/force/dominate: The compete/force/dominate style is characterized as, "I win, you lose." Often when one party feels they have a significant advantage, they will give the other party a final "take it or leave it" offer or there is no deal. This style is also appropriate when one party has a better BATNA – that is, best alternative to a negotiated agreement.

Consider the following scenario: The Canadian Auto Workers union threatened a strike in late 2002 that would have crippled Ford Motor Company's ability to provide engines for their hot-selling Ford vehicles. What happens if agreement is not reached? The worse case scenario would be that agreement cannot be reached and a work stoppage ensues. If Ford had plants in other parts of the world that could supply the needed engines then they would have the best fall-back position – i.e., settlement not reached and Ford continues to produce and sell vehicles. Since they have alternative sources of supply and the autoworkers do not have comparable sources of income, Ford's BATNA is substantially better than that of the CAW. On the other hand, if Ford does not have alternative sources for engines, then it might appear that the union has the advantage – the best alternative to a negotiated agreement. If Ford did not accede to the union's demands, the union would strike and final assembly of the hot-selling vehicles in the U.S. would be curtailed.

Our analysis of previous negotiations between Midwest Plastics and Local 1243 lead us to conclude that the parties did not use good communication skills to gain understanding of the other side's needs. The forcing style used by both parties has fostered long-term resentment and contempt for their adversaries.

Collaborative/integrate/problem solve: The collaborative/integrate/problem solve style is usually characterized as, "I win, you win." In essence, collaborative negotiations means that you must seek to determine what the other side really wants, then find a way or show them how to get the desired item. At the same time, you can get what you want. This style gives you an opportunity to question the other side to ascertain their interests and needs. Joint problem solving leads all parties to understand the issue and consider constraints. Solutions are developed collaboratively, and mutual trust and respect can be primary gains of this style. Although this style of negotiations is ideally best, it tends to be the most time consuming. Also, not every issue or demand can be resolved as "win – win" solutions. Some negotiations clearly have winners and losers.

It has been our experience with the Labor Agreement negotiations simulation that many students try to win all they can for their side. We contend that effective negotiations occur only when both sides realize that labor and management have a responsibility for the survival of each other. Thinking must shift to where the participants want to "create value" for all corporate stakeholders. That is, both parties approach negotiations wanting to develop a win-win situation.

Source: Adapted with permission from Edwin C. Leonard, Jr., and Raymond L. Hilgert, Supervision: Concepts and Practices of Management, ninth edition (Cincinnati, OH: South-Western College Publishing/Thomson Learning, 2004), pp. 576-577 (http://leonard.swlearning.com).

For a comprehensive overview on negotiating and resolving conflicts, see Roger Fisher, William Ury, and Bruce Pattor, *Getting to Yes: Negotiating Agreement Without Giving In*. (New York, Penguin Books WA, 1991); and Professor Edward G. Wertheim's website (http://web.cba.neu.edu/~ewertheim/interper/negot3.htm)

NOTES TO STUDENTS

1. For suggestions on how to improve your negotiating skills and knowledge prior to beginning the Labor Agreement Negotiations simulation, see the following sources:

Herb Cohen, *You Can Negotiate Anything* (New York: Bantam Books, 1980),
　　　Chapter 7: Winning at all costs
　　　Chapter 8: Negotiating for mutual satisfaction
　　　Chapter 9: More on the Win-Win technique

Roger Fisher, William Ury, & Bruce Patton, *Getting to Yes: Negotiating Agreement Without Giving In, Second Edition.* (New York Penguin Books USA, 1991),
　　　Chapter 6: What if they are more powerful? (Develop your BATNA – Best
　　　　　　Alternative to a Negotiated Agreement)
　　　Chapter 7: What if they won't play? (Use negotiation jujitsu)
　　　Chapter 8: What if they use dirty tricks? (Taming the hard bargainer)

Roger Fisher and William Ury, *Getting to Yes: Building a Relationship That Gets to YES* (Boston: Houghton Mifflin Company, 1988),
　　　Page 65:　We can't resolve differences without understanding them.
　　　Page 115: Help them perceive our conduct as trustworthy.
　　　Page 136: Negotiators often use coercive tactics.
　　　Page 143: Focus on positions vs. Explore interests.
　　　Page 145: Either/or vs. Multiple options.
　　　Page 160: But what if....

Gary Karrass, *Negotiate to Close: How to Make More Successful Deals* (New York: A Fireside Book/Simon & Schuster, Inc., 1985),
　　　Part II. (Chapters 11, 12, 13): Tactics for Handling Tactics
　　　Chapter 16: Making Concessions
　　　Chapter 23: Tactics to Watch Out For

R. J. Lewicki, *Negotiation*, 3rd edition (Homewood: IL: McGraw-Hill Irwin, 1997).

Charles S. Loughran, *Negotiating a Labor Contract: A Management Handbook*, 2nd edition (Washington, D.C.: BNA Books, 1992).

Edward Wertheim, *Negotiations and Resolving Conflicts: An Overview.* (http://web.cba.neu.edu/~ewertheim/interper/negot3.htm).

2. Just about every branch of the federal government has its own Web site. And most offer sub-sites with important information. FirstGov at www.firstgov.gov is an excellent one-stop access point for all U.S. government resources. Enter phrases and keywords to help find specific information.

3. View the Bureaus of National Affairs (BNA) Web site: http://laborandemploymentlave.bna.com. If your college, university or company subscribes to the service, we suggest you review the following:

- Chapter on Duty to Bargain: This Chapter discusses the duty to bargain, subjects that fall within its scope, bargaining information, exceptions to and enforcement of the duty, and bargaining obligations under special circumstances.
- Collective Bargaining Negotiations and Contracts Manual:
- CBNC 8 – Negotiating Contracts
- CBNC 10 – Compensation (Also see BNA's Wage Trend Indicator. Subscribers to BNA's Daily Labor Report and Daily Report for Executives receive the Wage Trend Indicator as part of their subscription.
- CBNC 18 - Wage & Economic Data
- CBNC 100- Sample Clauses: How to Use

4. Visit the AFL-CIO Web site (www.aflcio.org) to view the following topics:

- How & Why People Join Unions
- About the AFL-CIO
- Working Families Agenda
- Common Sense Economics
- Safety & Health on the Job
- Working Women
- Executive Pay Watch
- Worker's Rights
- Speeches, News Releases & Testimony

 # NOTES